Seashore Life of Florida and the Caribbean

Seashore Life of Florida and the Caribbean

Gilbert L. Voss

DOVER PUBLICATIONS, INC.
Mineola, New York

Bibliographical Note

This Dover edition, first published in 2002, is an unabridged republication of the revised and enlarged work published by Banyan Books, Inc., Miami, Florida, in 1980. The original work was published by E. A Seemann Publishing, Miami, Florida, in 1976.

DOVER *Pictorial Archive* SERIES

Library of Congress Cataloging-in-Publication Data

Voss, Gilbert L.
   Seashore life of Florida and the Caribbean / Gilbert L. Voss.
      p. cm.
   Originally published: Rev. and enl. ed. Miami, Fla. : Banyan Books, 1980.
   Includes bibliographical references (p.).
   ISBN 0-486-42068-X (pbk.)
   1. Marine invertebrates–Caribbean Area–Identification. 2. Marine inverte-
brates–Florida–Identification. 3. Seashore animals–Caribbean Area–Identification
4. Seashore animals–Florida–Identification. 5. Seashore plants–Caribbean
Area–Identification 6. Seashore plants–Florida–Identification. I. Title.

QL134.5 .V67 2002
592.177'365—dc21

                                                                    2001054298

Manufactured in the United States of America
Dover Publications, Inc., 31 East 2nd Street, Mineola, N.Y. 11501

To Nancy, Rob, and Linda

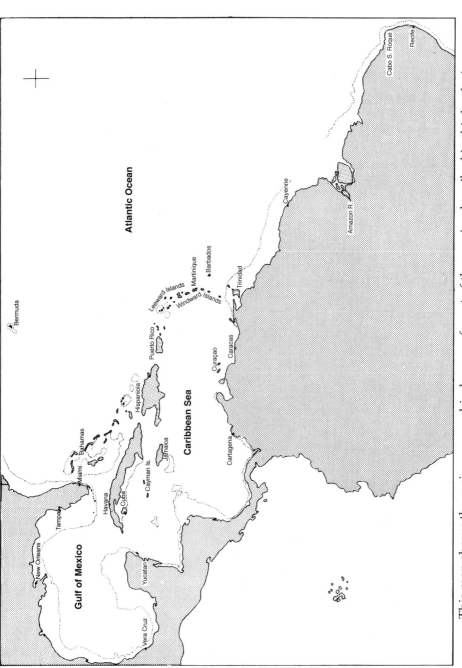

This map shows the major geographical range of most of the species described in this book. A few species extend further north and south, while others are more restricted to tropical waters.

Contents

Preface

This book is intended to serve as a guide to the identification of the common invertebrate animals, exclusive of shelled mollusks, of the West Indian Marine Province. The species included represent only a small part of the total fauna but are those that one might reasonably expect to find on a day's trip to the seashore or the coral reefs. They therefore are the larger, more conspicuous species of the shore and shallow water down to a depth of about 50 ft. (15 m).

The West Indian Marine Province embraces the tropical waters of the Western Atlantic. It includes the Bermuda Islands, the southern part of Florida from Miami to about Tampa, the Bahama Islands, and the mainland and islands of the Caribbean southward to about São Paulo, Brazil. This vast region is one of varied habitats from mangrove swamps to grass beds, sandy and muddy beaches, and coral reefs. Its marine life is very rich, numbering in the tens of thousands of species, and a guide to the total fauna would require several large, stout volumes.

The sandy beaches of the Atlantic coast north of Miami belong to the familiar Carolinian Province; several excellent volumes, such as Roy Waldo Miner's *Field Book of Seashore Life* and that delightful book, *The Sea-Beach at Ebb-Tide* by Augusta Foote Arnold, are available. For our tropical waters, however, no general guide has so far been presented to the public. For the Mollusca several excellent books are available, such as *American Seashells* by R. Tucker Abbott and *Caribbean Marine Shells* by Warmke and Abbott. Because of their general availability, and to introduce the reader to the other fascinating animals of the shore, the mollusks have been excluded from this volume.

The invertebrate phyla are arranged in the order of their supposed evolutionary progression from the Protozoa, or single-celled animals, to the echinoderms. Although strictly speaking the tunicates are not invertebrates, they are included because guides to the marine vertebrates usually are restricted to the fishes. Within the phyla, the breakdown is by class, order, and family, below which the species descriptions are given.

The descriptions are written in language as simple as possible; where technical terms are required, they are explained in the text or in the accompanying illustrations. Only obvious characters are used for identification, necessitating at most the use of a magnifying glass or simple hand lens. Color is given where significant. The sizes are those of the average adult; young animals may be much smaller, and some adults will attain larger sizes. Measurements are given in both inches and feet and in their metric equivalents. In calculating millimeters, centimeters and meters, the figures are rounded off so that they will not appear more precise than the inches and feet from which they were taken. Significant characters and colors are indicated in the accompanying figures, which usually are found on the page facing the species description. The geographic ranges given are general, but it must be understood that when a species is stated to occur from Bermuda southward to Brazil that does not imply that it is to be found on every island in between.

In groups containing many genera and species, several species possibly may resemble the one described and illustrated. Where similarities may occur, for instance in the brittle stars and crustaceans, the reader is warned that for positive identification it may be necessary to have access to the specialized scientific literature or to consult a specialist. A partial list of pertinent scientific publications on each group appears in the bibliography.

My hope is that this book will make your trip to the seashore both more enjoyable and more informative. If it accomplishes either of these objectives, the book will have been worth the work to produce it.

I have been a student of tropical marine invertebrates for over 30 years and have collected and explored much of the area covered here. No one person, however, can be familiar with all the diverse forms of marine invertebrates. Fortunately, I have the friendship and assistance of a number of noted invertebrate specialists. Foremost of these is Dr. Frederick M. Bayer of the University of Miami and the Smithsonian Institution. He has read the entire manuscript. Dr. Donald R. Moore, Dr. Lowell P. Thomas, and Robert Work, all from the University of Miami, have also read the manuscript and made many valuable suggestions as to the species to be included. Without the assistance of these and other colleagues too numerous to mention here, this volume would have been much more difficult to write; it is the richer for their help.

The pen and ink drawings are all drawn by me. Some are drawn from actual specimens whereas others are redrawn from a wide variety of original scientific publications. The color plates originally appeared in *Sea Frontiers*, the publication of the International Oceanographic Foundation (IOF). Grateful thanks are given to Dr. F. G. Walton Smith, president of IOF, and Mrs. May Smith, managing editor of *Sea Frontiers*, for their permission to use the material. Finally, I wish to thank my daughter, Linda Voss, for her dedication and patience while typing the numerous drafts and final manuscript. My wife Nancy is due a special word of thanks for her infinite patience and understanding while the work was in progress and her valuable criticism of the artwork.

About the new edition

The first edition of this book dealt with the marine invertebrates of the tropical Western Atlantic exclusive of the shelled mollusks. More than 300 drawings illustrated over 250 species. This new edition not only revises the original text but adds over 80 genera and species of common marine algae, sea grasses and strand plants. All species are illustrated by me either from life or redrawn from scientific publications.

Although marine plants, particularly the algae, have been dealt with scientifically in two recent monographs, no work of a popular nature on the tropical algae of our area has been published. The plant additions, found on page 153 and the following pages, will make this book truly representative of the seashore life of Florida and the Caribbean.

The new material on collecting and preserving algae will be found at the end of the plant section. Artistically mounted algae are even being displayed at art shows; the section on preservation will initiate the novice into this interesting and instructive hobby.

In preparing this revision of my book I have benefited from the advice of my friend Lt. Col. Corrine Edwards, USAF (Ret.), one of our most vigorous and informed students of Florida seashore life. For her enthusiastic support of and interest in this book I extend my most grateful thanks.

University of Miami
1980

GILBERT L. VOSS
Professor of Biological Oceanography and Curator of Marine Invertebrates, Rosenstiel School of Marine and Atmospheric Science, University of Miami

Collecting and Preservation

Undoubtedly, one of the main reasons why shell collecting is so popular is the ease with which the day's take can be cleaned and preserved. A few minutes of boiling suffices to loosen the animal; it can be removed and discarded and, *voilà!* the specimen is ready to be identified, labeled, and relegated to the cabinet. With most of the other invertebrates, however, the problems are much greater.

In the first place, collecting is more of a problem. Most of the animals described in this book are somewhat secretive, burrowing into mud, sand, or even rock thus requiring much digging or hammering to pry them out, or they may retreat into algal mats or coral rubble from which they can be extracted only with much effort. Others sting or pinch and some are very swift runners, such as the crab Sally Lightfoot. Thus the collector may need to go into the field armed not only with pail and screw-top jars, but with rock hammer, stout-bladed knife, dip net, and shovel. A small beach seine and a push net are valuable assets.

Equipped with these tools (and a friend to carry them), a discerning eye, and an inquisitive mind, a wide diversity of invertebrates will become your captives. Here another problem arises! What do you do with them? My advice is to keep the specimens in a jar or bucket of seawater, watch them, observe their movements and colors, perhaps identify them without ruining your book by getting it soaked with salt water, and finally turn them loose to go their ways back to their homes.

If closer examination is required, the collection should be sorted out to be sure that only those desired are retained, duplicates and unwanted specimens returned to the sea, and only the remainder taken home. These specimens are best studied either by keeping them alive in an aquarium, examining them fresh in seawater in a white porcelain pan, or by preserving them permanently either dried or in one of the liquid preservatives.

Many of the animals described and illustrated in this book make excellent aquarium residents. Care must be exercised that only compatible animals are kept together; many rare specimens otherwise may disappear during the night, eaten by one of the other inhabitants. Only experimentation will reveal the proper food to be used and the compatibility of the specimens. Some animals, for example, corals and alcyonarians, are very difficult to maintain without special aquarium set-ups.

Because of the great variety of types of animals included in this guide, various methods of preservation are needed. Some hard-shelled types may be dried; soft-bodied animals almost always require liquid preservation. Sea anemones and others are strongly retractile and unless narcotized will draw up into a fleshy glob if placed directly in preservative.

The most commonly accessible narcotizing agent is Epsom salts. The animal to be narcotized is placed in a clean glass or porcelain tray or dish (contact with bare metal will cause most animals to contract), covered with salt water, and allowed to expand fully. Then either crystals of Epsom salts or a saturated solution in seawater is slowly introduced into the dish until the animal gives no response when touched. It is then killed by very slowly introducing either alcohol or formalin until the animal is dead. It is then fixed in the proper preservative and transferred to an appropriate-sized jar and labeled.

Three major types of preservatives are used: formalin, ethyl alcohol, and isopropyl alcohol. Formalin is a saturated solution of formaldehyde gas in water. When purchased over the counter at a drugstore, U.S.P. formaldehyde is a 38 to 40% solution of formaldehyde gas in water but is 100% formalin. To make a 10% solution — as is most often used for preservation—mix one part of U.S.P. commercial formaldehyde with nine parts of water. The fumes are strong, so formaldehyde should not be used extensively in a closed room.

Two types of alcohol may be used; ethyl and isopropyl. Ethyl alcohol (ethanol) is preferred in museums and is used at 70% with freshwater. It is expensive. Although 70% ethanol is recommended, isopropyl alcohol is comparatively inexpensive and has the added attraction that it is used at 40% solution, so much less is required. It may have some deleterious effects upon some specimens, but it is becoming more popular even in the big museum collections.

Because of the varying consistency, fragility, chemical composition, contractability, and other characters of invertebrates, a variety of different methods are used in their preservation. The following preservative methods will be found useful for most purposes.

Sponges will rot and give off strong odors if they are not properly preserved. Specimens should be preserved in either 70% ethanol or 40% isopropyl alcohol. They may later be dried or retained in the preservative.

Jellyfishes are best preserved in either 5 or 10% formalin. Corals should be killed in freshwater and the flesh allowed to rot. It can then be washed away with a water jet and the skeleton dried and bleached in the sun. Sea anemones are difficult to expand and preserve, and their colors soon fade away. If one is determined to try, the anemone should be placed in seawater in a clean glass or china dish or bowl and left to expand. It may then be narcotized with Epsom salts and finally killed and fixed by the gradual introduction of formalin. At the last moment it may still contract and all the work will be in vain. If you are successful, final preservation is in 10% formalin. Alcyonarians may simply be dried in the shade.

Ctenophores are so fragile that little success in preservation has ever been attained. A 4 or 5% formalin solution sometimes works.

Flatworms are delicate and highly contractile. They are best preserved by placing them in a dish with just a little seawater and, when fully expanded, suddenly covering them with hot Bouin's solution. Final preservation is either in Bouin's or in 10% formalin. Bouin's solution gives off very disagreeable fumes. It may be obtained by consulting your druggist, a friendly chemist, or your nearest biological laboratory.

Annelids should be fixed in 10% formalin to harden the tissues and then transferred to 70% ethanol or stronger to prevent softening and disintegration.

Mollusks offer a variety of problems. Most soft-bodied opisthobranchs are best preserved by narcotizing with Epsom salts or magnesium chloride and then preserved in 70% ethanol. Octopus should be killed in freshwater, fixed with arms straight in 10% formalin for 48 hours or more, and then transferred to 70% ethanol. Squids should be placed directly in 10% formalin for 48 hours and then transferred to 70% ethanol.

Crustaceans may be preserved either wet or dry. If kept in preservative, they should be killed in freshwater to prevent their throwing off their legs and claws and then transferred to 70% ethanol. If they are to be dried, the same procedure should be followed, but after soaking in alcohol they can be laid out on absorbent paper, arranged in a lifelike manner, and thoroughly dried. When drying is complete, for best protection they should either be dipped or sprayed with plastic for permanence.

Starfish and brittle stars may be preserved dried. In order to dry them, starfish should first be soaked in 10% formalin for 24 hours and then dried in the shade. Brittle stars should be killed first by replacing seawater with a 3% solution of Epsom salts in freshwater. When dead, they should be transferred to 10% formalin for 24 hours and then dried in the shade. If either starfish or brittle stars are to be kept in liquid, they must be preserved in 70% ethanol. Formalin, even buffered with borax, will dissolve the calcareous plates and spines. Holothurians should be narcotized or put directly into 70% ethanol.

After the specimens have been preserved, they must be properly labeled. Although labels may have little or no value to some collectors who have several specimens only for their oddity, unlabeled or improperly labeled collections have no scientific value.

The label should be made of a heavy, 100% rag-content paper so that it will not disintegrate in the preservative. It should have written upon it, in either india ink or soft black lead pencil, at least the following information: scientific name of the species, the name of the describer, the locality where it was collected, the date collected, the name of the collector, and the name of the person who identified it.

I would be remiss if I did not here give a word of caution to the collector. Our shallow water marine life is faced with many difficulties: overcollecting; mindless killing; pollution; and the destruction of the habitats by dredging, filling, and bulkheading. It is incumbent upon us all to take no more specimens than are actually needed and to leave the collecting area in the same condition as we found it. This means filling in places we have dug out, turning back into their original positions large stones and logs overturned in our search, and leaving no litter of our own to mark our passing. Hopefully others may then find the same enjoyment when retracing our footsteps as we did when first we passed along the beach.

For information on collecting and preserving algae, see page 153.

Classification

The number of kinds of living animals far exceeds a million species. Very few of these have common names or are even known to anyone but a specialist in a particular group. For many years great confusion existed in attempts to bring order to the ever-increasing multitude of names, but in 1758 the Swedish naturalist Linnaeus proposed his famous binomial system of nomenclature. This system provided that each species be given two names — a generic name, always capitalized, and a specific name, which is never capitalized. The generic name shows affinity with other such species, the specific name the distinctness of each kind from all other kinds. The two names together comprise the name of the species, thus *Callinectes sapidus*, the blue crab. The names of genera and species are usually italicized.

In order to assist in research and bibliographic work, the name of the species is followed by the name of the person who first described it, thus *Callinectes sapidus* Rathbun. If the species is subsequently placed in a different genus from that in which it was originally assigned, the author's name is placed in parentheses. Thus the crab we know as *Cronius ruber* (Lamarck) was originally described as *Portunus ruber* by Lamarck.

Over the years a hierarchy of classification developed to put order in the animal and plant kingdoms and to show supposed relationships and evolutionary lineages. This hierarchy usually consists of the categories phylum, class, order, family, genus, and species. Only species names are lowercase. In some groups, such as the Crustacea, the relationships are so involved that a more complicated classification is required.

Phylum Arthropoda
  Class Crustacea
    Order Decapoda
      Suborder Reptantia
        Section Brachyura
          Subsection Brachygnatha
            Superfamily Brachyrhyncha
              Family Portunidae
                Subfamily Portuninae
                  Genus *Callinectes*
                    Species *sapidus* Rathbun

According to the International Rules of Zoological Nomenclature, the scientific names of animals are to be either Latin or, if in another language such as Greek, they are to be Latinized or treated as if they were in Latin. Most scientific names are descriptive, that is, they stress an important character, habits, geographical area where found, or bear an honorific name of a person, ship, or place. Thus an interpretation of the classification just given for the blue crab, *Callinectes sapidus,* is somewhat as follows.

Phylum —animals possessing jointed legs
  Class—having a shell
    Order—with ten legs
      Suborder—crawlers
        Section—short tail
          Subsection—short jaws
            Superfamily—short snout
              Family—idae, the family ending on the name
                of Portunus, Roman god of the harbor
                Subfamily—inae, the subfamily ending
                  Genus—beautiful swimmer
                    Species—savory, good eating.

A knowledge of Greek and Latin can often bring scientific names to life and can be informative as well as educational. Unfortunately few of us today have had a classical education. For those who wish to be able to translate the meanings of the names they encounter, the best book for the purpose is *A Source-book of Biological Names and Terms* by Edmund C. Jaeger, Charles C Thomas, Publisher, Springfield, Illinois.

This short discourse on names and classification will assist you in the use of this book and serve as an introduction to a fascinating field of study, a subject originated by Aristotle, brought into a semblance of order by Carolus Linnaeus, given a theoretical basis by Charles Darwin, and refined and multiplied by thousands of workers down to our day all striving to describe and name the living world around us.

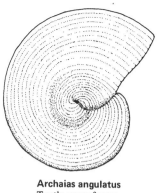

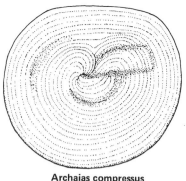

Archaias angulatus
Turtle grass foram

Archaias compressus
Button foram

Phylum Protozoa

The protozoans are mainly minute animals, each consisting of a single cell or of cells joined together to form colonies. They swarm in the seas, and microscopic examination of a drop of water or a scraping from a rock or piling will usually reveal an example. Most protozoans are free living, but some are attached or sessile, and some are protected by a skeleton of hard material such as silica or lime. Among the latter are the Foraminifera, which have a platelike shell of calcium carbonate with many small pores through which they extend their pseudopodia for feeding. Only a few species in our area are large enough to be seen easily by the naked eye.

CLASS SARCODINA

Order Foraminifera

FAMILY SORITIDAE

Turtle grass foram   *Archaias angulatus* (Fichtel & Moll.)
    The shell or test is about 1/4 in. (6 mm) in diameter, white, and coiled, the last chamber ending abruptly, forming an indentation in the side of the disk. This foram is very common on turtle grass blades where it is easily seen and collected.

Button foram   *Archaias compressus* (d'Orbigny)

    The test is thin and flat, nearly circular in outline, formed of tightly coiled series of chambers. It is about 1/4 in. (6 mm) in diameter and is found, like the preceding species, attached to turtle grass blades in shallow water. These forams are very numerous.

FAMILY HOMOTREMATIDAE

Red foram   *Homotrema rubrum* (Lamarck)

The red forams form small splotches or spots of dark to bright red, calcareous growths on such hard objects as dead corals, mollusk shells, and rocks. The growth usually has one or more projections from the surface. This species is found growing in the reef tract from the sea surface to considerable depths.

Homotrema rubrum (on a shell)
Red foram

Phylum Porifera
The Sponges

Sponges are sessile animals that grow attached to shells, stones, and other hard objects on the bottom. The living animal is formed of simply organized cells usually supported by a skeleton of fibers called spongin and calcareous or siliceous spicules, spicules alone, spongin alone, or it may have no skeletal structures. The outer skin is often very tough but is permeated by small pores through which water is pumped into the animal to filter out microscopic-sized food. The water is discharged through larger pores or holes called oscula. Reproduction is by fragmentation, budding, or the production of eggs and sperm.

The sponges found cast onto the beach are but the skeletons of former living animals and bear little resemblance to living sponges. Sponges are often amorphous with no distinct shape but some species grow in regular patterns. Thus identification usually requires microscopic examination of spicule preparations; only those species with characteristic growth patterns can be determined by eye alone.

Sponges grow in all types of habitats from intertidal rocks to the deep sea. Most are of no commercial value, but bath sponges are much sought after, being taken by hand with sponge hooks on long poles or by divers. Cleaned natural sponges still demand high prices in the markets; for many purposes they cannot be replaced by synthetics. Although there are several classes of sponges, only the class Demospongea is treated here.

CLASS DEMOSPONGEA

These sponges exhibit a great variety of shapes, sizes, and coloration. The skeleton may consist of spongin, siliceous spicules, both, or neither. There is a number of orders.

ORDER KERATOSA

This order contains those sponges that have only spongin as a skeleton, with no spicules, and a few, small sponges with no skeletal structures. This order includes the well-known bath sponges.

FAMILY SPONGIIDAE

Cuban reef sponge, Reef sponge   *Spongia obliqua* Duch. & Mich.
The reef sponge is usually black, nearly spherical, and has a fairly smooth surface. It grows on the reef tract and because of its low commercial value was formerly common. It was decimated by the sponge disease and is now rather rare in Florida. It occurs sporadically throughout the Caribbean.

Sheepswool sponge   *Hippiospongia lachne* (de Laubenfels)
The sheepswool is one of our most important commercial sponges and derives its name from the unusual softness of the cleaned skeleton. It grows in irregular but massive form with large, raised oscula. The thin, tough skin and strong sponge fibers make the sponge difficult to detach from the bottom without a knife or sponge hook. It is usually dull drab to black in color and may attain a diameter of several feet. It occurs widely in our area on suitable bottom but is becoming difficult to find due to overfishing.

Bleeding sponge   *Oligoceras hemorrhages* de Laubenfels
The colonies vary greatly in shape and size but commonly grow to a height of 4 to 5 in. (10 to 13 cm). It is dull to glossy black, very soft, and spongy. When squeezed or damaged, it gives off a blood red or cerise liquid. It grows in shallow water on hard bottom.

Cake sponge, Loggerhead (Bahamas)   *Ircinia strobilina* (Lamarck)
The colony is typically cakeshaped. It grows to a diameter of about 1-1/2 ft. (0.5 m) and is usually black but may be dull black or even gray if partly shaded. It has a very soft, spongy texture when wet but becomes hard and stiff when dry. Do not confuse the common name used in the Bahamas with the loggerhead sponge of Florida, an entirely different species.

Stinker sponge   *Ircinia fasciculata* (Pallas)
This is a very variable species in both shape and color. It attains a height of about 12 in. (30 cm). The surface is tough and the fresh animal is spongy, but it dries out to a hard consistency. It is brownish to brownish yellow, nodular, lobal, or branching and has conspicuous dark oscula. As the name implies, it may give off a very strong, somewhat unpleasant odor.

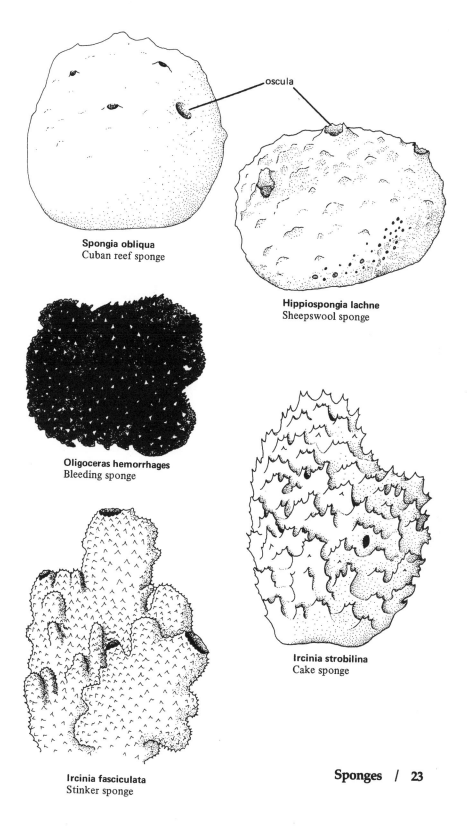

Spongia obliqua
Cuban reef sponge

oscula

Hippiospongia lachne
Sheepswool sponge

Oligoceras hemorrhages
Bleeding sponge

Ircinia strobilina
Cake sponge

Ircinia fasciculata
Stinker sponge

Vase sponge   *Ircinia campana* (Lamarck)
   The vase sponge, as the common name implies, is most often shaped like a vase or an inverted cone with a deep interior cavity; it may also be bell-shaped, as the scientific name *campana* denotes. It attains a height of 3 ft. (1 m) or more. The surface is somewhat rough and often coarsely to finely ribbed. In life it is spongy, but it becomes hard when dry. It is reddish to reddish brown in color.

Candle sponge   *Verongia fistularis* (Pallas)
   The typical animal is cylindrical, hollow, and candle size 3 to 12 in. (8 to 30 cm) or more. The surface is somewhat rough with only a few holes; it has a spongy texture when alive, but when dry it is stiff, brittle, and black. When living it is yellow, but when dying the sponge first turns blue violet and then black.

Branching candle sponge   *Verongia longissima* (Carter)
   This species is similar to the preceding one, but it is branching and never hollow. It is a duller yellow than *V. fistularis*; when dying it darkens but never turns black. It is commonly found in sprawling masses in shallow grass beds and around reefs.

FAMILY DYSIDEIDAE

Heavenly sponge   *Dysidea etherea* de Laubenfels
   This delicate little sponge seldom attains a height of more than a few inches (cm), but it may branch and form large colonies. It is soft and fragile when alive but brittle when dry. The living animal is sky blue in color and cannot easily be mistaken for any other sponge. It is common in grass beds and around reefs.

ORDER HAPLOSCLERINA

   This order contains a great variety of noncommercial sponges.

FAMILY HALICLONIDAE

Red sponge   *Haliclona rubens* (Pallas)
   The brick red to bright red, cakelike or branched colonies are commonly found in reef areas, in back reef lagoons, or among turtle grass. This species has a spongy consistency when alive. Because of their red color these harmless sponges are often confused with several red, stinging species. In general, all red or orange sponges should be avoided.

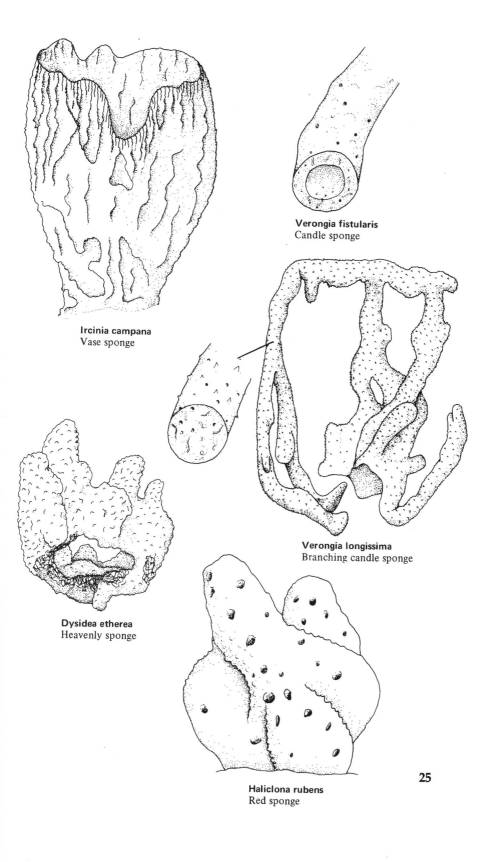

Ircinia campana
Vase sponge

Verongia fistularis
Candle sponge

Verongia longissima
Branching candle sponge

Dysidea etherea
Heavenly sponge

Haliclona rubens
Red sponge

25

Green sponge   *Haliclona viridis* (Duch. & Mich.)
   The green sponge is amorphous, incrusting, or slightly branched. It has a soft, spongy consistency and is easily torn apart. It is light grayish green to bright green when alive but fades when preserved. The colony may have a diameter of 4 to 5 in. (10 to 13 cm).

FAMILY DESMACIDONIDAE

Purple bleeding sponge   *Iotrochota birotula* (Higgin)
   This sponge is slenderly branching; the surface is covered with small, conical, pointed projections. It is deep purple but in sunlight has a thin yellow green surface sheen. When squeezed or pressed it exudes a rich purple juice.

Do-not-touch-me sponge   *Neofibularia nolitangere* (Duch. & Mich.)
   The colony is irregularly massive and covered with lobes or nodules with an osculum at the top of each protuberance. The color is drab to mahogany brown with a pale interior; the internal consistency has been described as similar to wet bread. It often grows on the reef at the base of colonies of the coral *Acropora*. This species is highly toxic; if handled with bare hands, it may cause severe burning and blistering, which may take days to disappear. The specific name, *nolitangere*, "do-not-touch," is in this case very appropriate.

Sprawling sponge   *Neopetrosia longleyi* (de Laubenfels)
   This common species grows in shallow water where its branching form spreads over the bottom rather than standing upright. It has a smooth yellowish green to dark olive green exterior with a lighter green interior. It has few spongy characteristics, and the branches break easily.

FAMILY CALLYSPONGIDAE

Tube sponge   *Callyspongia vaginalis* (Lamarck)
   The clustered, open-ended tubes in groups of up to six or more are commonly found on the beaches after stormy weather, They may attain a height of over 3 ft. (1 m). The individual tubes may have a diameter of up to 2 in. (5 cm). Occasionally the colonies are solid. The color is usually drab or pale bluish gray, often with a lavender tinge. They grow from shallow water to considerable depths.

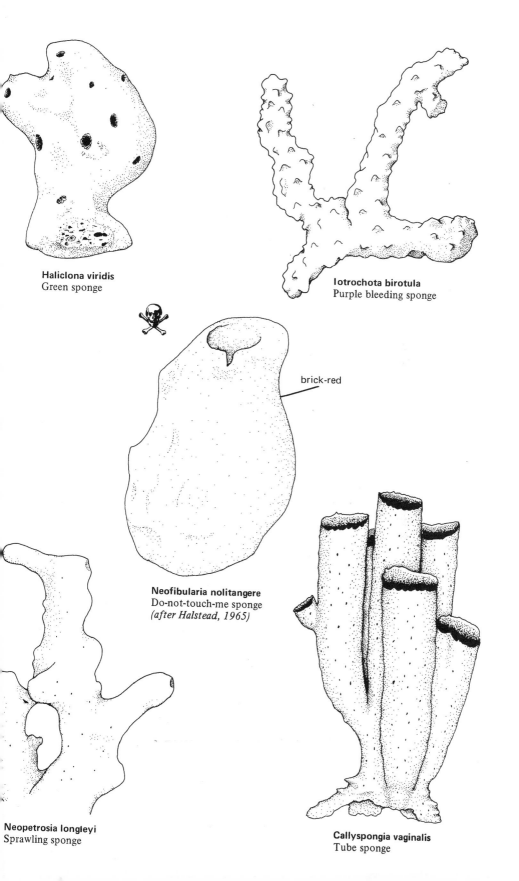

Haliclona viridis
Green sponge

Iotrochota birotula
Purple bleeding sponge

brick-red

Neofibularia nolitangere
Do-not-touch-me sponge
(after Halstead, 1965)

Neopetrosia longleyi
Sprawling sponge

Callyspongia vaginalis
Tube sponge

ORDER POECILOSCLERINA
FAMILY TEDANIIDAE
The Fire Sponges

Fire sponge   *Tedania ignis* (Duch. & Mich.)
This species grows in colonies 4 to 12 in. (10 to 30 cm) in height; the colonies are amorphous to massive with a smooth surface. The sponge is soft, fragile, and easily torn. The surface is bright red or orange but somewhat lighter colored inside. This sponge is highly toxic to most people and causes painful burns and rashes similar to a bad case of poison ivy. It is best never to touch bright red or orange sponges with the bare hand. This sponge is very abundant in bays and lagoons.

ORDER HADROMERINA
FAMILY CHOANITIDAE

Loggerhead sponge (Florida)   *Spheciospongia vesparia* (Lamarck)
Manjack (Bahamas)
The loggerhead is one of the largest species of sponge known, growing to a diameter of more than 3 ft. (1 m) and a height of more than 2 ft. (0.6 m). It is usually cakeshaped with a flat top that has a central depression. It has a hard, almost woody consistency, and has no commercial value. It is dark brown or black but is usually coated with bottom sediments that give it a grayish appearance except for the dark cluster of holes (oscula) at the top. It is a refuge for a host of marine animals, particularly snapping shrimp, which live in its internal tubes and passages. Do not confuse this species with the loggerhead sponge of the Bahamas.

FAMILY CLIONIDAE

Red boring sponge   *Cliona lampa* de Laubenfels
There are several poorly defined species of *Cliona* in our range. *Cliona lampa* excavates galleries about 1/16 in. (1.5 mm) in diameter in calcareous material, such as mollusk shells. It only protrudes from the galleries at the opening of an osculum. When a "sponge sucked" shell is broken open, the sponge tissue of *lampa* is bright orange or red.

ORDER EPIPOLASIDA
FAMILY TETHYIDAE

Golf ball sponge   *Tethya diploderma* Schmidt
This species and its relatives form spherical colonies the size of golf balls or smaller, with a reticulate surface composed of tightly packed clusters of

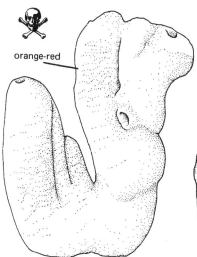

orange-red

Tedania ignis
Fire sponge

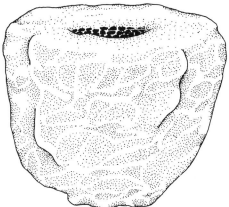

Spheciospongia vesparia
Loggerhead sponge

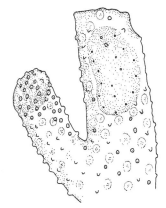

Cliona lampa
Red boring sponge

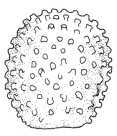

Tethya diploderma
Golf ball sponge

Sponges / 29

tubercles. The surface color varies from greenish to orange, but the inside color is always orange or a shade of orange or yellow. It commonly grows in shallow water in and around reefs or in grass beds. There are several very closely related species.

ORDER CHORISTIDA
FAMILY GEODIIDAE

White sponge   *Geodia gibberosa* Lamarck
The colony is massive, rounded, and up to 10 in. (25 cm) high. The surface is smooth, dirty white, and hard, with small clusters of pinprick-sized holes. It is occasionally overgrown by the soft-textured green sponge *Haliclona viridis*. It grows in shallow water, often in turtle grass beds.

ORDER CARNOSA
FAMILY CHONDRILLIDAE

Chicken liver sponge   *Chondrilla nucula* Schmidt
The chicken liver sponge has a remarkable likeness to chicken livers in size, appearance, and surface. It forms incrusting sheets on turtle grass leaves and other submerged objects. The color is grayish white mottled with dark gray or black. The sponge is rather firm with a very slick, smooth surface. It is very common in shallow grass beds and around coral reefs.

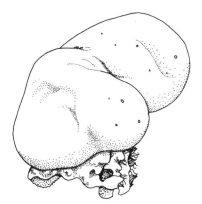
Chondrilla nucula
Chicken liver sponge

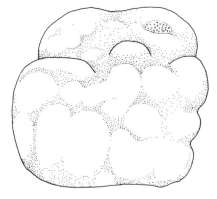
Geodia gibberosa
White sponge

Phylum Coelenterata
Jellyfishes, Hydroids, Corals, Sea Anemones, Sea Feathers, and Fans

The Coelenterates are radially symmetrical animals that possess a simple internal cavity. They range from sessile organisms, such as corals with only a larval planktonic stage, to pelagic animals, such as the large jellyfish and the colonial siphonophores represented by the Portuguese man-of-war. Many have a peculiar alternation of generations — a sessile asexual stage from which new individuals are formed by budding—and a pelagic sexual stage with normal reproduction.

A primary character of all Coelenterates is the possession of peculiar structures called nematocysts. These are ovoid or cylindrical capsules containing within them a coiled, sharp, often spinous thread. When the nematocyst comes into mechanical or chemical contact with a predator or prey, it is everted and the thread penetrates the organism, injecting a poisonous or paralytic fluid. Such organisms as the Portuguese man-of-war may inflict very painful stings.

The Coelenterata are divided into three classes: the Hydrozoa containing the hydroids and small jellyfish; the Scyphozoa containing larger jellyfish; and the Anthozoa containing the corals, sea anemones, and gorgonians.

CLASS HYDROZOA
ORDER LEPTOMEDUSAE
FAMILY SERTULARIIDAE

Stinging hydroid   *Macrorhynchia philippina* (Kirchenpauer)
This, and several closely related and almost indistinguishable species, is commonly found in shallow water growing on rocks, dock pilings, and

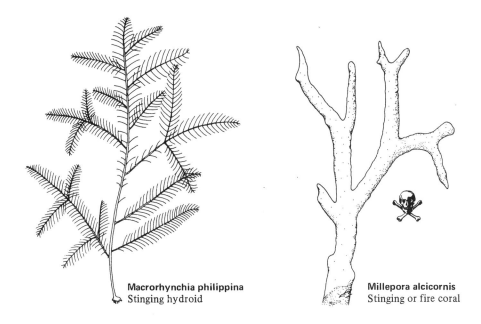

Macrorhynchia philippina
Stinging hydroid

Millepora alcicornis
Stinging or fire coral

marine grasses. Many of these hydroids cause painful stings if toxin is injected by the nematocysts. The pain may last for several days and require treatment by a physician. The colonies are often mistaken for marine plants.

ORDER MILLEPORINA

The colonies of this order form heavy calcareous skeletons much resembling corals, with which they were long classified.

FAMILY MILLEPORIDAE

The Stinging or Fire Corals

Stinging or fire coral   *Millepora alcicornis* (Linnaeus)

There are several species of *Millepora* in our area, all difficult to identify. The colonies may incrust alcyonarian skeletons or form upright, thick, ruffled sheets or small branches. When alive the colony is brown to light creamy yellow with white tips. The surface is smooth, covered with minute pores within which the polyps live. Contact with a live colony may cause severe burning sensations due to toxins injected by the nematocysts. Fire corals are found on coral reefs throughout the West Indies.

ORDER SIPHONOPHORA

This order contains free-swimming colonies of individuals of different kinds, each kind specialized for different purposes—swimming, feeding, digestion, reproduction. In some groups all the individuals are small and form long chains; in others one or more groups form large floats supporting the other individuals.

SUBORDER CYSTONECTAE

These siphonophores float at the surface by means of a large, inflated float.

FAMILY RHIZOPHYSALIIDAE

Portuguese man-of-war   *Physalia physalis* (Linnaeus)

Swimmers and beachcombers often encounter this beautiful but dangerous animal either floating on the surface like a violet balloon or washed up on the beach where the float makes a popping sound if stepped upon. Alive or dead they should be handled with care because full contact can cause pain severe enough to send a person into shock. If severely stung, one should consult a physician at once. The violet float may exceed 6 in. (15 cm) in length. Attached to this are long fishing tentacles, armed with powerful stinging cells, that may trail out behind as much as 60 ft. (18 m). The species is found in all tropical seas.

SUBORDER DISCONECTAE

Siphonophores with a large, disclike float.

FAMILY VELELLIDAE

By-the-wind sailor   *Velella velella* (Linnaeus)

The delicate, violet, colonial animal forms a thin, elliptical float about 2 in. (5 cm) long and 1 in. (2.5 cm) wide bearing a low, transparent crest or sail set at an angle across the disc. Numerous small fishing tentacles are suspended beneath the float. This species often washes up onto tropical Atlantic beaches in great numbers.

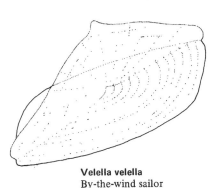

Velella velella
By-the-wind sailor

Physalia physalis
Portuguese man-of-war

tentacles

Blue buttons   *Porpita linneana* (Lesson)
    This siphonophore forms a thin, pale blue, round, flat disc about 1 in.
(2.5 cm) in diameter, fringed with delicate blue tentacles. It is common on
tropical beaches but often overlooked because of its delicate shading and
small size.

CLASS SCYPHOZOA

The Jellyfishes

ORDER SEMAEOSTOMEAE

The mouth is quadrate with four, long, oral lobes.

FAMILY ULMARIDAE

Moon jellyfish   *Aurelia aurita* (Lamarck)
    The moon jellyfish has a thick transparent disc or umbrella with pink-
ish, cordlike gonads. The disc may have a diameter of over 1 ft. (30 cm); it is
fringed with fine, white tentacles with stinging cells that may cause
temporary burning sensations if touched. It is commonly washed ashore
along much of our range. It has an almost worldwide distribution.

Upside-down jellyfish   *Cassiopeia xamachana* (Bigelow)
    This unusual jellyfish is found in West Indian and Florida waters in
stagnant or semistagnant areas lying upside down on the bottom. Its
brownish or yellowish disc is about 6 to 12 in. (15 to 30 cm) in diameter. The
area around the mouth is formed of clusters of brownish or greenish,
grapelike bodies that contain cultures of symbiotic algae. The jellyfish lies
upside down in order to provide the necessary sunlight for their growth.
We presume that the jellyfish uses the algae as food, either directly or
indirectly.

ORDER RHIZOSTOMEAE

Cannonball jellyfish   *Stomolophus meleagris* (L. Agassiz)
    The body (umbrella) is shaped like the half of an egg and has a diameter
of about 7 in. (18 cm). The bell is milky bluish or yellowish, shading into
brown near the border.
    It is thick and strong and a good swimmer.

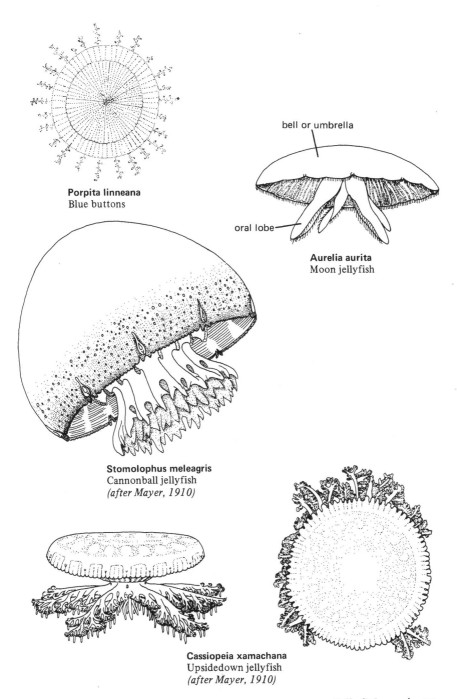

Porpita linneana
Blue buttons

bell or umbrella

oral lobe

Aurelia aurita
Moon jellyfish

Stomolophus meleagris
Cannonball jellyfish
(after Mayer, 1910)

Cassiopeia xamachana
Upsidedown jellyfish
(after Mayer, 1910)

Jellyfishes / 35

CLASS ANTHOZOA

Gorgonians, Anemones, and Corals

SUBCLASS OCTOCORALLIA

ORDER GORGONACEA

Members of this order form an important part of the reef and hard bottom communities of the West Indian region. With only a few exceptions, the colonies of polyps form a hard, horny or calcareous, central branching skeleton. The cups (calyces) in which the polyps live are formed of spicules of various shapes, sizes, and color, which are the main basis for identification.

The submarine forests of sea feathers, whips, and fans are characteristic of West Indian reefs, and a view of their soft colors, waving with the motion of the sea, is unforgettable. The colonies are host to many other animals that live on or among them, such as the flamingo tongue shell, *Cyphoma;* the delicate lavender *Neosimnia;* the purple shrimp, *Tozeuma;* and the basket starfish, *Astrophyton.* Gorgonians are widely sold in the curio trade, and at least one yields prostoglandin, an important pharmaceutical product.

FAMILY BRIAREIDAE

Common Briareum, Corky sea fingers   *Briareum asbestinum* (Pallas)
The body of the colony is fingerlike and has a woody to spongy texture. When the polyps are contracted the surface is smooth to nodular with numerous small calyces (pores). In life it is purplish gray with expanded polyps. Dried out, the skeleton is brownish, yellowish, or grayish. It occurs in reef areas.

FAMILY PLEXAURIDAE

Black sea rod, Prostoglandin Plexaura   *Plexaura homomalla* (Esper)
This species forms bushy colonies, which are flattened and branched laterally and dichotomously. The terminal branchlets are up to 4 in. (10 cm) long and 1/8 to 1/5 in. (3 to 5 mm) wide. The surface is nearly smooth. The colonies are yellowish brown when living but turn dark brown to nearly black when dried. It is important pharmaceutically. This species occurs on the reef tract from Bermuda through the West Indies.

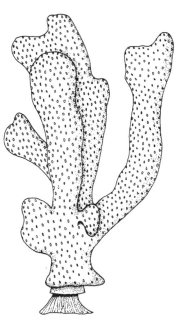

Briareum asbestinum
Common Briareum,
Corky sea fingers

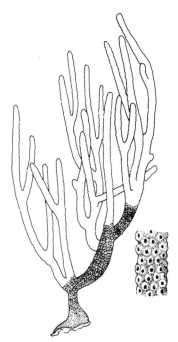

Plexaura homomalla
Prostaglandin Plexaura
Black sea rod

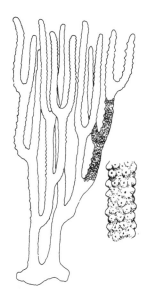

Plexaura flexuosa
Bent Plexaura *(see page 38)*

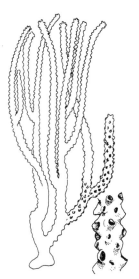

Eunicea palmeri
Palmer's Eunicea *(see page 38)*

Sea Feathers and Fans / 37

Bent Plexaura, Sea rod   *Plexaura flexuosa* Lamouroux

This very common species occurs in a number of forms. Small colonies branch in a single plane, but larger ones become bushy although still somewhat flattened. The surface is smooth except for a small raised lip beneath each calyx. The colonies vary in color from white to yellow, varying shades of brown, and reddish purple to purple. They are common throughout our range. *(See drawing on page 37)*

Palmer's Eunicea   *Eunicea palmeri* Bayer

The colonies have very soft and flexible, long, slender branches about 1/8 in. (3 mm) in diameter and up to 10 to 11 in. (25 to 28 cm) long. The branches are slightly knobbed and irregular on the surface and are in one plane in young colonies but bushy in older ones. Fresh specimens are purplish gray, grayish brown, or brown; dry specimens are brown. It is at present known only from the Florida reefs. *(See drawing on page 37)*

Mammillated Eunicea   *Eunicea mammosa* Lamouroux

This pale yellowish brown species grows mostly in a single plane, the branches project laterally and are dichotomously branched. The surface is covered with rather closely set, tubular to mammiform calyces that are directed upward. It grows in reef areas and shallow water.

Warty Eunicea   *Eunicea calyculata* Ellis & Solander

The colonies are tall with cylindrical, stout terminal branches having a diameter of 1/3 to over 1/2 in. (8 to 13 mm). The surface is covered with gaping calyces, each surrounded by a low, rounded lip. The color is yellowish brown in life, drying to light to dark brown. It lives in coral reef areas.

Double-forked Plexaurella   *Plexaurella dichotoma* (Esper)

The colonies are bushy, dichotomously branched, the ends of the branchlets 1/3 to 1/2 in. (8 to 13 mm) in diameter. The branchlets may be tall and straight or short and crooked according to the habitat. The surface is covered with low, round to more often slitlike pores. The color is light brown to yellowish.

Gray Plexaurella   *Plexaurella grisea* Kunze

The colonies are similar to those of the preceding species, but the branches are few, stand stiffly erect, and are more slender. The margins of the pores may be slightly elevated, but the general surface appears smooth and grayish.

Eunicea mammosa
Mammillated Eunicea

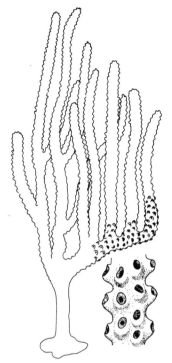

Eunicea calyculata
Warty Eunicea

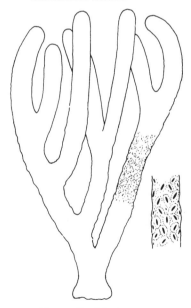

Plexaurella dichotoma
Double-forked Plexaurella

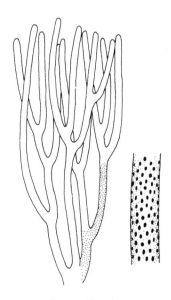

Plexaurella grisea
Gray Plexaurella

Sea Feathers and Fans / **39**

Spiny Muricea   *Muricea muricata* (Pallas)
   The colonies are small, grow in a single plane, and are broad and fanlike. The calyces are tubular and formed of stiff spicules, which give the colony a spiny appearance. The branches are characteristically flattened at the points of branching. The living colony is light colored, drying to grayish white or pale yellow brown.

FAMILY GORGONIIDAE

Bipinnate sea feather   *Pseudopterogorgia bipinnata* (Verrill)
   The colony is erect, pinnately branched in one plane, with the branchlets bipinnately branched and evenly spaced along the main stem. The twigs are flattened with a double row of alternating, slitlike pores along the edges. The color in life is violet, occasionally yellow or whitish. It lives on reefs or rocky bottoms in shallow water.

Purple sea plume, Dry sea plume   *Pseudopterogorgia acerosa* (Pallas)
   The colony is large, plumose, with long, often drooping branches. The surface of the colony has a rather dry, fine sandpaperlike feel even when under water. The color is bluish gray, purple, or yellow. It grows to a height of 3 ft. (1 m) or more. It lives in shallow reef and reef flat areas. It and the following species are the two most common West Indian sea plumes.

Slimy sea plume   *Pseudopterogorgia americana* (Gmelin)
   This species is very similar to the preceding one, forming large, bushy, plumose colonies with long, drooping branchlets. It is bluish gray or purplish in color. In contrast to *P. acerosa* it feels slimy and can produce large amounts of mucus that cause the branches to stick together when dried. It is common in the reef habitat.

Bahamian sea fan, Venus fan   *Gorgonia flabellum* Linnaeus
   This is perhaps the best-known species of gorgonian in the West Indian region. It forms a fan-shaped colony of closely anastomosing branchlets which result in a network. The colony is usually gray to pale violet or blue but may occasionally be yellow. It attains a height of about 2 to 3 ft. (0.6 fo 1 m). The branchlets are compressed at right angles to the main axis of the fan. It is rather uncommon in Florida.

Common sea fan   *Gorgonia ventalina* Linnaeus
   The colony is very similar to that of the preceding species except that the branches and branchlets are compressed in the plane of the fan and not at right angles to it. The color is yellow or purple, occasionally whitish. It is common in the Florida Keys.

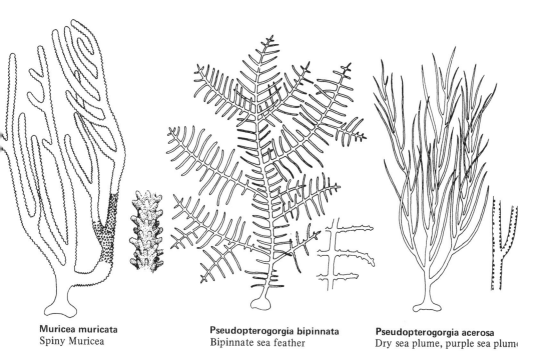

Muricea muricata
Spiny Muricea

Pseudopterogorgia bipinnata
Bipinnate sea feather

Pseudopterogorgia acerosa
Dry sea plume, purple sea plume

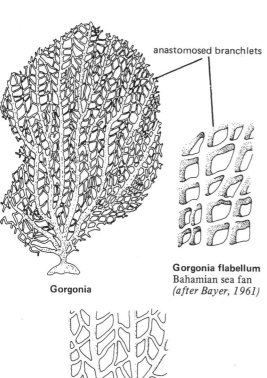

anastomosed branchlets

Gorgonia

Gorgonia flabellum
Bahamian sea fan
(after Bayer, 1961)

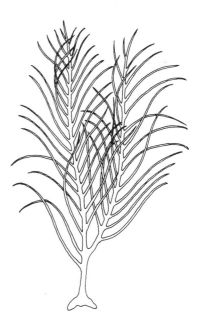

Pseudopterogorgia americana
Slimy sea plume

Sea Feathers and Fans / 41

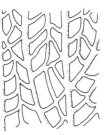

Gorgonia ventalina
Common sea fan
(after Bayer, 1961)

Yellow sea whip   *Pterogorgia citrina* (Esper)

The colony is low and sparsely branched. The branches are flattened. The polyps lie along the edge of the branches in separate, slitlike calyces. The colonies are usually yellow, sometimes olivaceous gray, with reddish purple calyces. The species lives in shallow water attached to hard bottom, often unassociated with reef habitats.

Angular sea whip   *Pterogorgia anceps* (Pallas)

Colonies are bushy, more profusely branched than those of the preceding species, and larger. The branches and branchlets appear to be double-folded, resulting in three or four edges to the branches. The polyps lie in closely set calyces within a narrow groove along the edges of the branches. The color in life is usually brownish purple but may vary through olive green or gray to dull yellow. It lives in somewhat deeper water than *P. citrina*. A somewhat similar species, *P. guadalupensis*, also has the polyps in grooves, but it has broad, flat branches.

ORDER PENNATULACEA
FAMILY RENILLIDAE
The Sea Pansies

Common sea pansy   *Renilla reniformis* (Pallas)

The frond is little wider than long, thick and fleshy. The fleshy stalk is longer than the radius of the frond. The polyps are found only on the upper surface of the fronds. The color is rose or pale purple. Some have a white or yellow frond and a deep purple stalk. They are found in shallow water in sandy areas. The species is distributed from Cape Hatteras and Florida to South America but does not occur in the Gulf of Mexico.

Müller's sea pansy   *Renilla muelleri* Kölliker

This species is similar to the preceding one, but the frond is broader than long and the stalk is shorter than the radius of the frond. The color is white to deep purple. It occurs from the Gulf of Mexico southward to Brazil.

SUBCLASS ZOANTHARIA
The Sea Anemones and Corals
ORDER ACTINIARIA

Sea anemones are among the most beautiful of our seashore life and are favorites with saltwater aquarists. The typical sea anemone has a tubular

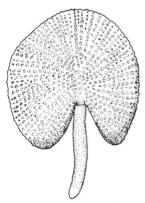

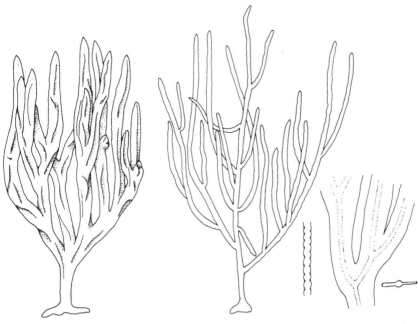

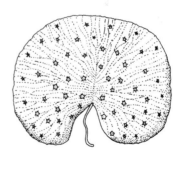

Pterogorgia anceps
Angular sea whip

Pterogorgia citrina
Yellow sea whip

P. guadalupensis
Flat sea whip

Renilla reniformis
Common sea pansy

Renilla muelleri
Müller's sea pansy

body that is closed and flattened into a suction base at the bottom while the top is surrounded by tentacles and closed into a slitlike mouth. Although internally the cavity is partially divided by vertical partitions (septa), because of the slit mouth, the animal is biradially symmetrical.

Both the body column and the tentacles are highly contractile, the animal withdrawing and contracting at the slightest disturbance or alarm. The tentacles are armed with stinging cells (nematocysts) that in some species may be quite toxic. Anemones are sessile, attaching by their disc to hard substrates over which they may slowly glide as necessity dictates. They are sexual animals, reproducing by eggs and sperm, but they may also bud off new individuals or a single animal may separate by transverse fission into two new individuals.

Sea anemones filter other organisms from seawater by their tentacles or kill larger animals that come into contact with them. They are also noted for maintaining close commensal relationships with hermit crabs and various small shrimp and even fish.

FAMILY ACTINIIDAE

Pink-tipped anemone   *Condylactis gigantea* (Weinland)

This is the largest and showiest sea anemone in the tropical western Atlantic. It may attain a diameter across the tentacles of over 1 ft. (30 cm). It attaches itself to rocks or other hard objects, such as concrete bulkheads and pilings. The colors are variable according to habitat; the column may be pale blue, whitish, or even vivid orange or light red, but the tentacles are always tipped with either pink or blue. It is common on the reef or in shallow grass beds.

Warty sea anemone   *Bunodosoma cavernata* (Bosc)

The warty sea anemone is recognized in the field mainly by its color and sculpture. The rather muscular column is closely set with vesicles that are

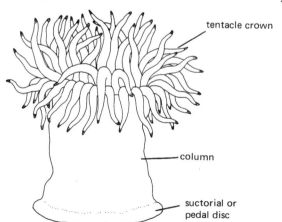

tentacle crown

column

suctorial or pedal disc

Condylactis gigantea
Pink-tipped anemone *(after McMurrich, 1889)*

Bunodosoma cavernata
Warty sea anemone
(after Duerden, 1902)

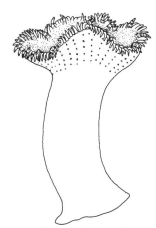

Phymanthus crucifer
Speckled anemone
(after McMurrich, 1889)

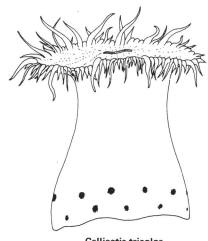

Calliactis tricolor
Tricolor anemone

arranged in vertical rows and give it a warty appearance. The column is very variable in color, ranging from olive green to muddy brown with reddish vesicles. The tentacles are splotched with light yellowish green and dark olive green. The area around the mouth is usually reddish to scarlet. This anemone is active and fully expanded at night; during the day it is often contracted, appearing only as a reddish lump.

FAMILY PHYMANTHIDAE

Speckled anemone   *Phymanthus crucifer* (Lesueur)
This small, brown anemone is common in shallow water where the brownish speckled pattern offers an excellent camouflage with the gravel and rock among which it lives. The colors and patterns, however, are variable. The base is often attached to a buried object, and, when the animal retracts, it may withdraw from view completely.

FAMILY HORMATHIIDAE

Tricolor anemone   *Calliactis tricolor* (Lesueur)
The tricolor anemone is very variable in color ranging from drab brown to dark orange and red or purple. Whatever the color, there is usually a series of small, dark spots around the outer edge of the basal plate. This anemone is often found growing on mollusk shells inhabited by large hermit crabs; often more than one anemone is living on the same shell. Apparently the stinging cells help protect the hermit crab, and the anemone obtains more food than it would find attached to a rock.

Sea Anemones / 45

FAMILY AIPTASIIDAE

Pale anemone   *Aiptasia pallida* (Verrill)

These small anemones attain a height of only about 2 in. (5 cm), with slender columns and few long tentacles. They are pale gray or whitish, nearly transparent, and are often overlooked. They grow on rocks or other hard objects in shallow water.

Ringed anemone   *Bartholomea annulata* (Lesueur)

The column or stalk is rather broad but short. The numerous tentacles are long and often drooping. The stalk is brownish. The tentacles are light brown and ringed along their entire length with pale brown or white. It grows on or under rocks or other hard objects.

ORDER ZOANTHIDEA

This order contains organisms resembling sea anemones, but the individual polyps are united by a basal tube or stolon.

FAMILY ZOANTHIDAE

Mat anemones   *Zoanthus pulchellus* (Duch. & Mich.)

These grow in thick, matlike colonies of greenish or bluish sea anemone-like individuals. The colonies are usually found attached to rocks just below the low tide mark. The colonies may be reduced in size or disappear seasonally. Another smaller species, *Z. sociatus,* is more commonly found growing in sandy areas. They occur throughout our range.

Knobby zoanthidean   *Palythoa mammillosa* (Ellis & Solander)

The colonies form thick, incrusting mats on dead coral in the reef zone. The skeleton is hard, somewhat corklike in consistency. The outer surface is covered with large, round calyces surrounded by a low, rounded ridge or lip. The fleshy polyps have short, stout tentacles, and when the polyps are extended the colony resembles the hard coral *Montastraea cavernosa.*

ORDER SCLERACTINIA

The Stony Corals

Coral polyps closely resemble sea anemones in general structure, and many of them live a solitary existence. Most, however, form small to massive colonies and all secrete a calcareous skeleton of varying patterns.

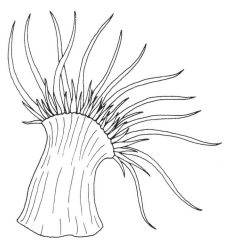

Aiptasia pallida
Pale anemone
(after Carlgren & Hedgpeth, 1952)

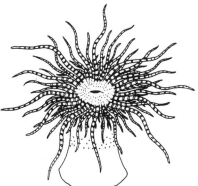

Bartholomea annulata
Ringed anemone
(after Duerden, 1902)

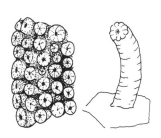

Zoanthus pulchellus
Mat anemone
(partly after Duerden, 1902)

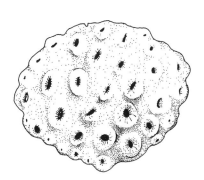

Palythoa mammillosa
Knobby zoanthidean

Sea Anemones and Stony Corals / **47**

In the tropics most solitary corals live in the deep sea; the few that dwell in Atlantic shallow water are insignificant.

The true reef-building or hermatypic corals have large branching or massive boulderlike skeletons, which over thousands of years may form extensive reefs or atolls. The coral skeleton is constructed by the slow deposition of calcium carbonate layers beneath the fragile polyp. The polyps are assisted in skeletal formation by minute, single-celled algae (zooxanthellae), which live within the tissues of the polyp and are themselves responsible for much of the coral's color.

Coral reefs afford a unique habitat in the sea. Because reef corals are tropical, they are found throughout the area covered by this book wherever ecological conditions permit. Many of the animals described here live in either permanent or temporary association with coral reefs. The reef habitat is one of the richest in the world in number and diversity of marine life.

SUBORDER ASTROCOENIIDA
FAMILY ACROPORIDAE

Elkhorn coral   *Acropora palmata* (Lamarck)
    The colony forms treelike structures of flat, expanded branches resembling the horns of a moose. The color is brownish yellow to cream, with the tips of the branches pale cream to white. The colony grows in exposed areas of the reefs and may attain a height of up to 10 ft. (3 m). It is one of the major characteristic corals of the West Indian region.

Staghorn coral   *Acropora cervicornis* (Lamarck)
    Brownish yellow or cream colored, the colonies form treelike clusters of round, slender branches, usually with pointed tips. The colony may attain a height of about 5 ft. (1.5 m), or it may assume a sprawling form, singly or in heaps on the reef tract. It occupies a somewhat more protected zone than the preceding species. It is a valuable commercial species in the tourist trade.

SUBORDER FUNGIIDA
FAMILY AGARICIIDAE

Lettuce coral   *Agaricia agaricites* (Linnaeus)
    Lettuce coral forms semicircular, flat sheets or ruffled, upright plates much resembling lettuce leaves. The plates are thick and crossed by raised lines or ridges between which are the pitlike calyces. The color is creamy yellow brown to purple brown with the base splotched with green. It often grows on the bases of the elkhorn coral.

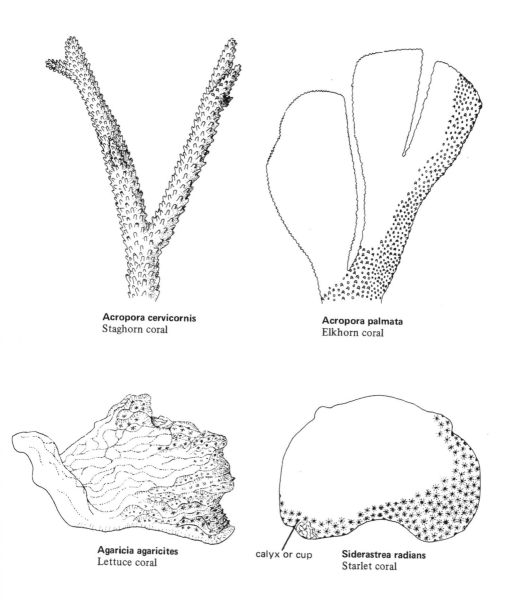

Acropora cervicornis
Staghorn coral

Acropora palmata
Elkhorn coral

Agaricia agaricites
Lettuce coral

calyx or cup   **Siderastrea radians**
Starlet coral

FAMILY SIDERASTREIDAE

Starlet coral   *Siderastrea radians* (Pallas)
    This coral forms small, rounded masses from a few inches to about 1 ft. (30 cm), in diameter. The individual calyces (cups) are small, about 1/8 in. (3 mm) across, deep and angular. The colony is yellow to brown to gray. A larger species, *S. siderea,* grows to a height of about 2 ft. (60 cm) and has larger, shallower cups. Both species occur in reef and associated areas.

FAMILY PORITIDAE

Clubbed finger coral   *Porites porites* (Pallas)
This species forms low, thick, yellowish-brown clumps of short, stout branches that are swollen or clubbed at the ends. The calyces are small, about 1/12 in. (2 mm) in diameter and shallow. The colonies are common in shallow water near shore where they may form extensive beds. Two other common forms occur: *P. divaricata,* with branches under 1/4 in. (6 mm) in diameter, and *P. furcata,* with branches as thick as *P. porites,* nearly 1/2 in. (13 mm) wide, but without clubbed ends. All range from Florida throughout the West Indies.

Porous coral   *Porites astreoides* Lamarck
The colony forms irregular, slightly mounded sheets of a yellow brown or greenish to neon green color. The colony often reaches a diameter of more than 2 ft. (.6 m). It may be incrusting or massive and is usually covered with small bumps. It occurs from Bermuda to Brazil.

SUBORDER FAVIIDA

FAMILY FAVIIDAE

Knobbed brain coral   *Diploria clivosa* (Ellis & Solander)
This species forms large, heavy, low growths with irregular knobs. The surface is covered with narrow, shallow, winding but unconnected grooves. The color is greenish brown in the valleys but chocolate colored on the surface. The polyp tentacles are greenish with white tips.

Brain coral   *Diploria labyrinthiformis* (Linnaeus)
The brain coral forms massive, boulder-size clumps 6 to 8 ft. (2 to 2.5 m) in diameter and height. In life it is brownish yellow. The surface is covered with narrow, deep, winding valleys that interconnect and resemble the convolutions of the human brain. It is abundant behind the fore reef.

Rose coral   *Manicina areolata* (Linnaeus)
This species is somewhat variable in color, ranging from brown to yellow to green with white tentacles. The skeleton is roughly elliptical, with pointed, narrow ends, somewhat flattened above, with a deep, irregular furrow. The bottom is irregularly conical, often with a short stalk. The young coral grows attached to the bottom, but when mature it eventually breaks off and lies free. It attains a length of about 6 in. (15 cm). It is a hardy coral for aquarium use.

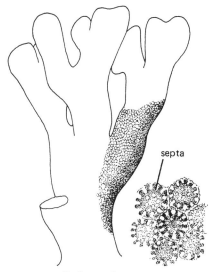

septa

Porites porites
Clubbed finger coral

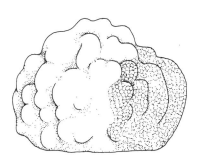

Porites astreoides
Porous coral

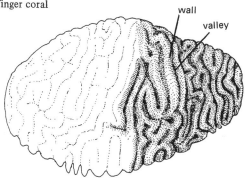

wall

valley

Diploria clivosa
Knobbed brain coral

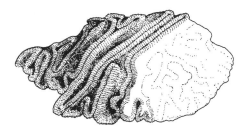

Diploria labyrinthiformis
Brain coral

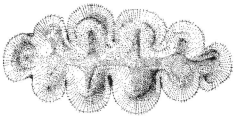

Manicina areolata
Rose coral

Stony Corals / 51

Large star coral   *Montastrea cavernosa* (Linnaeus)
    The colony forms large boulders up to and exceeding 5 ft. (1.5 m) across.
The coral is greenish yellow to brownish yellow. The surface is covered
with large, raised calyces 1/5 to 1/2 in. (5 to 13 mm) in diameter and rather
closely spaced. The ridges of the calyces (cups) extend over the lip and
onto the surface of the coral beyond the cups. It is an important reef
species.

FAMILY OCULINIDAE

Ivory bush coral   *Oculina diffusa* Lamarck
    This coral forms tightly branching colonies with a bushy appearance.
The branches are irregular, knobby, with few, widely spaced, large, shallow cups. The branches are slightly less than 1/2 in. (13 mm) in diameter. It
is abundant throughout our range but is seldom seen on the outer reef.

FAMILY TROCHOSMILIIDAE

Star coral   *Dichocoenia stokesii* Edwards & Haime
    The coral forms massive boulders over 1 ft. (30 cm) in diameter. The
surface is covered with round to oblong cups, unconnected, with walls
projecting above the common surface and closely crowded together. It
occurs in reef areas from Florida through the West Indies.

Pillar coral   *Dendrogyra cylindrus* Ehrenberg
    This species forms heavy, cylindrical branches or pillars up to 4 ft. (1.2 m)
long. It has narrow, winding valleys that are not all connected. The valleys
are separated by narrow walls. The coral is brownish yellow. It occurs on
the reef from Florida through the West Indies, usually in slightly deeper
water.

FAMILY MUSSIDAE

Large flower coral   *Mussa angulosa* (Pallas)
    The colony is formed of short, heavy branches, each ending in a large
cup. The overall appearance is roundish, boulderlike, up to several feet (1
m) across. The cups or short valleys may be up to 5 in. (13 cm) long and
nearly 2 in. (5 cm) wide. The septa are toothed, giving the cup a shaggy
appearance.

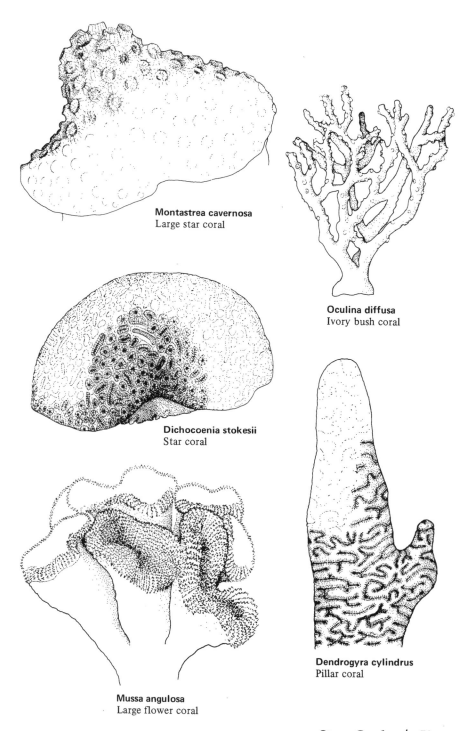

Montastrea cavernosa
Large star coral

Oculina diffusa
Ivory bush coral

Dichocoenia stokesii
Star coral

Mussa angulosa
Large flower coral

Dendrogyra cylindrus
Pillar coral

Stony Corals / 53

SUBORDER CARYOPHYLLIDA
FAMILY CARYOPHYLLIIDAE

Flower coral   *Eusmilia fastigiata* (Pallas)

This coral grows in small colonies with massive branches ending in cups that are more or less oval and up to 1-1/2 in. (4 cm) long, with sharp edges or rims. There are no teeth on the septa. The color is dark brown with greenish cups and white tentacles. It occurs from Florida throughout the West Indies.

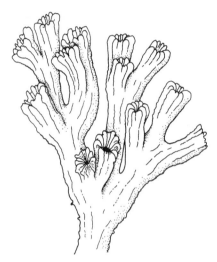

Eusmilia fastigiata
Flower coral

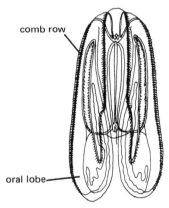

Mnemiopsis mccradyi
Lobate comb jelly
(after Mayer, 1912)

Phylum Ctenophora
The Comb Jellies

The comb jellies somewhat resemble jellyfish. They are very transparent and fragile. As a result they are almost never seen on the beach; at times, however, they may be quite common in shallow water where they may be sighted by swimmers. Often the comb jellies are first recognized by the shimmering lines of light reflected from their comb rows.

Ctenophores are characterized by the possession, in most, of eight rows of ciliated plates, or ctenes, by which they swim. Ctenophores can make little forward progress, but they may sink or rise in the sea by the beating of the rows of cilia (hairs). At the apex of the animal there is a small, transparent, bubblelike structure within which are four hairs with a granule balanced on their tips. By pressing harder upon one or the other hairs as the ctenophore tilts, the comb row is caused to beat harder thus righting the animal.

Comb jellies, despite their fragileness, are predators upon larval fish and fish eggs, often wreaking havoc with a year's spawning. Because of their delicate construction, ctenophores are difficult to collect and preserve. A number of species are in the open ocean, but only one is common in our inshore waters.

Lobate comb jelly   *Mnemiopsis mccradyi* (Mayer)
The animal is about 4 in. (10 cm) long, somewhat pear shaped, with two large, flaplike, oral lobes. The comb rows are prominent. The body is firm, transparent, and greenish amber in color; it may be brilliantly luminescent. This species is often seen in shallow water.

Phylum Platyhelminthes
The Flatworms

The flatworms are unsegmented, flattened, and very soft-bodied. Most are quite small and are so flat that they are difficult to capture except by use of a knife blade inserted beneath them. There is a head with eyespots. The mouth is located ventrally near the midpoint of the animal or at the anterior end. Locomotion is by beating of the numerous body cilia (hairs).

There are three classes: Turbellaria, Trematoda, and the Cestoda. The Turbellaria, the only one represented here, are free-living and common in the sea. Many are minute, but some may reach considerable size. They vary from drab, transparent animals to ones with strikingly gaudy colors. Few are seen on our seashores.

CLASS TURBELLARIA

Crozier's flatworm   *Pseudoceros crozieri* (Hyman)

This flatworm reaches a length of about 2 in. (5 cm). Its ground color is grayish brown crossed with numerous fine lines of dark brown. It is widely distributed in the West Indies.

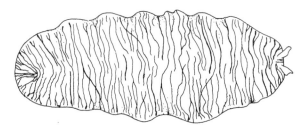

Pseudoceros crozieri
Crozier's flatworm
(after Zeiller, 1974)

Phylum Nemertea
The Ribbon Worms

The ribbon worms are cylindrical to somewhat flattened, highly contractile, soft-bodied, unsegmented worms. Most of them are small, but a few attain considerable size and may grow in excess of 20 ft. (6 m). Usually they are very slender and brightly colored. These animals are secretive, burrowing in sand or living in algal clumps or mats or in oyster shells.

Some ribbon worms have an unusual anterior proboscis equipped with a sharp spine that is used to capture prey. In some species this also injects a slightly toxic secretion that may cause swelling and temporary pain.

Nemertines have sexual reproduction; they may also reproduce asexually by fragmentation. The worms break easily when handled, and the separate parts may regenerate lost parts and form new complete individuals.

Ribbon worms are very common in the sea, dwelling from the shore to the greatest depth of the ocean trenches. Most require microscopic examination for identification; however, a few are recognizable by their size and color.

ORDER PALEONEMERTEA

FAMILY TUBULANIDAE

Black-ringed ribbon worm   *Tubulanus rhabdotus* Correa
The mature worm is about 10 in. (25 cm) long and very slender. The ground color is ochre green. Both the somewhat expanded head and the body are marked with black bands; the lighter parts have scattered black spots arranged in regular rows. Both the light portion and the black bands bear scattered, light-colored halos. *(See drawing on page 58)*

Florida ribbon worm   *Tubulanus floridanus* Coe

Similar in appearance to the preceding species, this animal attains a length of only about 1-2/3 in. (42 mm) but is very narrow with an expanded, heart-shaped head. It is brownish in color, with about 30 narrow transverse white bands or rings. It was described from Florida but probably occurs throughout the West Indies.

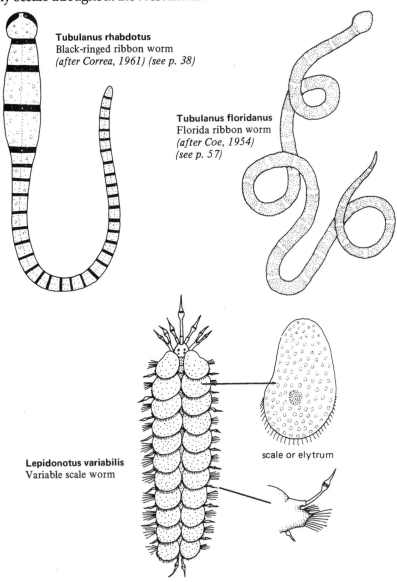

Tubulanus rhabdotus
Black-ringed ribbon worm
(after Correa, 1961) *(see p. 38)*

Tubulanus floridanus
Florida ribbon worm
(after Coe, 1954)
(see p. 57)

scale or elytrum

Lepidonotus variabilis
Variable scale worm

Phylum Annelida
The True Worms

CLASS POLYCHAETA

The polychaetes, which include most of the marine worms, are segmented animals. Each segment is somewhat repetitious of the others. The body segments bear swimming or crawling appendages and external gills. The anterior segment bears few to many tentacles used as sensory organs, tasting palps, and two to four eyespots. Some are blind. Beneath the head is the mouth, which in some species is armed with a pair of large, chitinous jaws.

Polychaetes hatch from the egg into a planktonic larva termed the trochophore, which metamorphoses into the worm stage. Adults occupy a variety of habitats. Some are free living predators on the bottom; others live in tubes of various types; many burrow into sand or mud bottoms.

Most of these worms are harmless; a few can bite, and some may give a very painful sting. Many are quite beautifully colored. A few are of considerable commercial importance as fish bait. They are found from the intertidal region to the greatest depths in the sea.

FAMILY POLYNOIDAE
The Scale Worms

Variable scale worm   *Lepidonotus variabilis* Webster

This small worm is about 1 in. (25 mm) long, bearing on its upper surface twelve pairs of round, leathery, overlapping scales. The scales (elytra) are fringed with short hairs on their outer margins and have a tuft of hairs on the inner posterior margin. The elytra are mottled gray or brown and are easily detached. In general the color is grayish or grayish brown with a white or dark spot over each scale scar. The species is found among oyster shells, in rubble, and in clumps of algae, especially *Halimeda*.

FAMILY AMPHINOMIDAE

Green bristle worm   *Hermodice carunculata* (Pallas)

The large, greenish worm is commonly found under stones or other hard objects in grass beds or on the reef. It may reach a length of nearly 10 in. (25 cm). It is easily recognized by its squarish body in cross section, greenish color, orange red gills, white bristles, and the large branched or folded caruncle (beard) on the surface of its head. It should be handled with care as the bristles are easily shed in one's hands and may cause very painful, long-lasting stings.

Orange bristle worm   *Eurythoe complanata* (Pallas)

This worm is similar to the greenish bristle worm but is somewhat more slender and attains a length of about 6 in. (15 cm). Its body is orange yellow; the gills tend toward a reddish color while the soft bristles along the sides are whitish. The caruncle on the top of the head is nearly smooth and unbranched. This species lives mainly on the reef flat and in rocky areas under stones or old coral heads. Like its counterpart just described, the bristles may painfully sting bare hands.

Red-tipped bristle worm   *Chloeia viridis* Schmarda

The red-tipped bristle worm attains a length of about 4 to 5 in. (10 to 13 cm) and a width across the bristles of nearly 2 in. (5 cm). It is elliptical with an irridescent body and fringed by large, separate bundles of strong, white bristles tipped or banded with bright orange or red. The caruncle is divided longitudinally into three ridges or lobes. This worm is a voracious predator and is often caught by hook-and-line fishermen after it has engulfed bait and hook whole. It occurs in somewhat deeper water than the preceding species, on open sand and mud bottoms.

FAMILY ONUPHIDAE

Shaggy parchment tube worm   *Onuphis magna* (Andrews)

Onuphis constructs a parchmentlike tube that is characteristically covered with pieces of shell, mangrove leaves, pieces of turtle grass blades, or other types of debris. There is only a single opening to the tube. The animal itself is long, slender, and not obviously modified for tube dwelling. It has rather long, branching, conspicuous gills, especially in the midregion of the body. It occurs in shallow water in sandy or muddy bottoms.

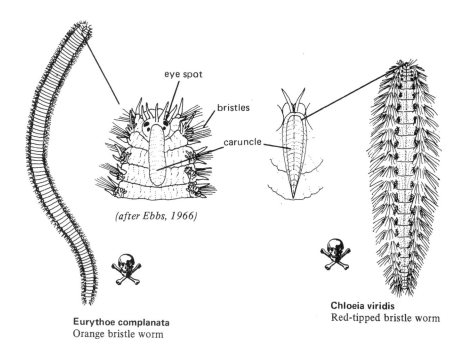

eye spot

bristles

caruncle

(after Ebbs, 1966)

Eurythoe complanata
Orange bristle worm

Chloeia viridis
Red-tipped bristle worm

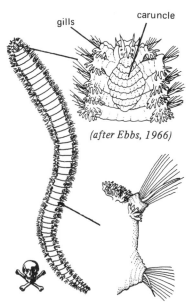

gills

caruncle

(after Ebbs, 1966)

Hermodice carunculata
Green bristle worm

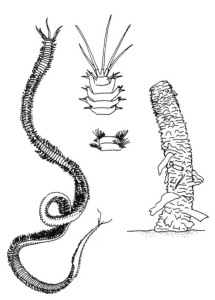

Onuphis magna
Shaggy parchment tube worm
(after Treadwell, 1921)

True Worms / **61**

FAMILY EUNICIDAE

Sponge worm   *Eunice denticulata* Webster
   This long, slender worm lives within a variety of sponges where it forms a thin, tough, parchmentlike tube which is so convoluted that whole worms are very difficult to extract. The animal attains a considerable size, as long as 2 ft. (61 cm), but is only about 1/5 in. (5 mm) wide. The anterior end of the worm is colored a bright vermillion, but this shade fades away posteriorly until the main part of the body is transparent or colorless except for the bright red bordering gills. There are five cirri or antennae on the head and a pair on the next segment.

Long bristle Eunice   *Eunice longisetis* (Webster)
   Similar in appearance to the preceding species, this worm is smaller, attaining a length of over 16 in. (41 cm). It is dark colored, the anterior part dark green shading to brown in the middle and purple posteriorly. The sixth segment, in contrast, is colorless or white. The tentacles on the head are banded either brown and white or purple and white. The two anal cirri are banded deep purple and white. This species lives in dead coral rubble.

Atlantic palolo   *Eunice schemacephala* Schmarda
   This is a long, slender animal attaining a length of over 2 ft. (61 cm). It is pale green and irridescent with the tentacles and cirri often a brownish hue. On reaching maturity, the sexual section of the males becomes coral pink, of the females sage green. When these parts are distended with eggs and sperm, the animals swarm at the surface of the sea, the sexual parts break off and burst, and the sexual products are released. This swarming takes place at the last quarter of the moon in June-July, although some swarming takes place the day before and the day after.

FAMILY CHAETOPTERIDAE

Parchment tube worm   *Chaetopterus variopedatus* (Renier)
   The tubes of this species offer the best identification. They are formed of a parchmentlike material in which sand grains are often imbedded and are U-shaped, with only the ends with the two openings projecting 4 or 5 in. (10 to 13 cm) above the surface of the mud or sand in shallow water. The animal is unusual. Its body is divided into three distinct parts: a large anterior end with normal segments bearing bristles and an expanded shovellike mouth, a midsection with large, paddlelike structures for pumping water through the tube, and a normal posterior section. The animal is capable of emitting strong bioluminescent flashes. The tubes are often washed out of the ocean bottom during storms and cast up in incredible numbers onto the shore.

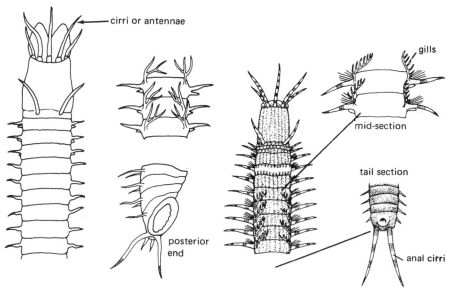

Eunice denticulata
Sponge worm
(after Treadwell, 1921)

Eunice longisetis
Long bristle Eunice
(after Treadwell, 1921)

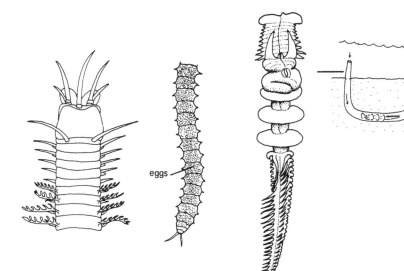

Eunice schemacephala
Atlantic palolo
(after Treadwell, 1921)

Chaetopterus variopedatus
Parchment tube worm

FAMILY ARENICOLIDAE

Lug worm   *Arenicola cristata* Stimpson

This large, stout worm burrows in sand or in sand and mud bottom forming a U-shaped burrow. The anterior end of the burrow is marked by a depression that the worm creates by engulfing quantities of sand from which it digests the organic particles and deposits the waste sand in a mound at the other end of the burrow. The animal is rather roughly sculptured, greenish to brownish green in color with brownish, red-tufted gills. There are seventeen setae-bearing segments. The worm grows to about 4 in. (10 cm). Its northern counterpart, *A. marina,* is widely distributed around the Atlantic.

FAMILY PECTINARIIDAE

Golden tube worm   *Cistenides gouldii* Verrill

The tubes of this species are slightly more than 1 in. (2.5 cm) long, conical, curved, and open at both ends. They are delicate and covered with a layer of sand. The animal is small and golden. They are common in quiet, shallow water on mud bottoms.

FAMILY TEREBELLIDAE

Medusa worm   *Loimia medusa* (Savigny)

The worm is soft-bodied, rather thick, and attains a length of about 6 in. (15 cm). It is grayish with whitish or pinkish bands. It has numerous long, very extensible tentacles that are greenish or bluish. It lives on or in the bottom or under objects in a chitinized tube covered with bottom debris. The tentacles may be extended outward along the bottom for several feet. When disturbed, the tentacles are rapidly withdrawn, seemingly disappearing into the bottom. It is widely distributed in the tropics.

FAMILY SABELLIDAE

Feather Duster Worms

Black-spotted feather duster   *Branchiomma nigromaculata* (Baird)

This small worm does not much exceed 1 in. (2.5 cm) in length. The body is speckled with dark spots, and there are black eyespots on the branchiae. This is a common species in shallow water from the Bahamas to Brazil.

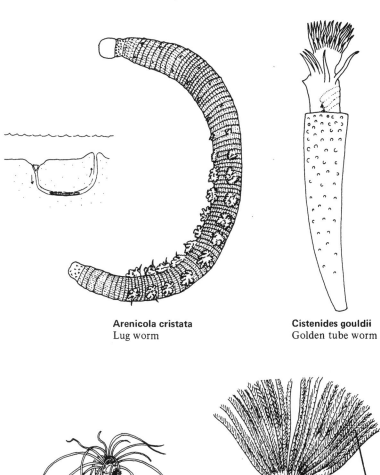

Arenicola cristata
Lug worm

Cistenides gouldii
Golden tube worm

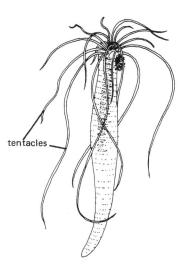

Loimia medusa
Medusa worm

tentacles

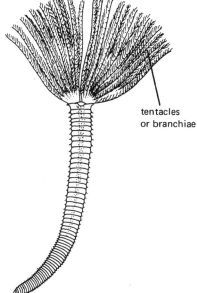

tentacles
or branchiae

Branchiomma nigromaculata
Black-spotted feather duster

Banded feather duster   *Sabella melanostigma* Schmarda

The banded feather duster somewhat resembles *Branchiomma nigro-maculata* except that the tentacles bear rather widely spaced, paired black eyespots and the tentacles have a few wide bands of dark red. It is well known from Bermuda throughout the West Indies.

Magnificent feather duster   *Sabellastarte magnifica* (Shaw)

This beautiful, large worm well deserves its name. It grows to a length of about 5 in. (13 cm), of which nearly 4 in. (10 cm) is the tentacular crown. The tentacles are colored shades of brown with several series of spots forming bands of brown with light tan spots, chocolate brown with white, dark purple with brown spots, or dark mahogany red banded with light brown. It is widely distributed in tropical shallow seas.

FAMILY SERPULIDAE

Horned feather worm   *Spirobranchus giganteus* (Pallas)

One of the showiest worms on the reefs, it forms a hard calcareous tube on the surface of dead coral or by penetrating living coral. The opening of the tube has a single, stout, sharp spine on one edge. The animal is about 4 in. (10 cm) long with a pair of spirally wound gills, each cone shaped with yellow to bright orange or red filaments. Near the bases is a short stalk bearing a nearly round whitish operculum used to close the mouth of the tube. From near one side of the operculum arises a widely spread double horn with a few short spikes on the outer parts. This worm is very sensitive to changes in light intensity and if disturbed snaps into the tube with only the operculum and double horns showing.

Star feather worm   *Pomatostegus stellatus* Mörch

The star feather worm forms a calcareous tube but without a protecting horn on its rim. The worm is slender, the body about 3 to 4 in. (7.5 to 10 cm) long with a double-folded set of gills or branchiae that may be variously colored, usually banded with shades of yellow and orange, white and black or maroon. The stalked operculum is composed of a series of separated round discs with finely spinous borders ending in a small cluster of spines arranged in a star shape. The species is very common in the reef tract.

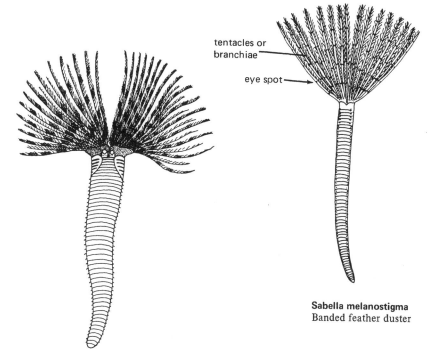

tentacles or
branchiae

eye spot

Sabella melanostigma
Banded feather duster

Sabellastarte magnifica
Magnificent feather duster

operculum

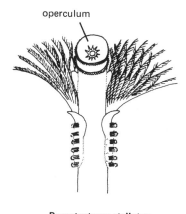

Pomatostegus stellatus
Star feather worm

operculum

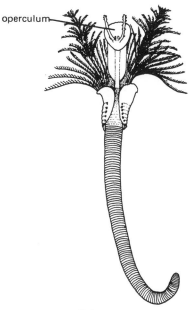

Spirobranchus giganteus
Horned feather worm

Phylum Sipunculida
The Sipunculid Worms

Sipunculid worms of the tropics are mostly small animals, many of which bore into soft rock or old coral; others inhabit mollusk shells or form their own tubes. The animal has no true segments or internal divisions but is essentially a muscular bag with an extrusible long neck, which is termed the introvert because it can be turned inward like the finger of a glove. The introvert may be covered on the outside by a series of small teeth by means of which it bores or hauls itself through the substrate. They are inconspicuous animals with a few species in our area.

Antillean sipunculid worm   *Phascolosoma antillarum* Grube & Oersted
    This species attains a length of about 2 in. (5 cm) when extended. It is brownish to rich chestnut brown, and the introvert is armed with teeth. It usually burrows in soft beach rock and may be very common. It lives in shallow water through the West Indies.

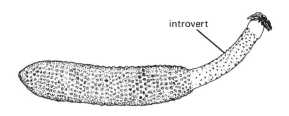

introvert

Phascolosoma antillarum
Antillean sipunculid

Phylum Bryozoa
The Moss Animals

The moss animals are minute creatures that form branching, erect, or incrusting colonies on a wide variety of plants and animals and such submerged hard surfaces as boat and ship bottoms, pilings, and floating objects. The animals and their shells are so small that they require a microscope for detailed examination. The creeping, incrusting colonies form white to pink or purple, delicate network traceries visible to the naked eye. In the incrusting forms each animal lives within a small shell which has an opening protected by a trap door that closes when the animal is withdrawn. The mouth is surrounded by a ring of tentacles by which the animal filters plankton and organic particles from seawater. The phylum is divided into two classes: the Entoprocta in which the anus lies near the mouth within the ring of tentacles and the Ectoprocta in which the anus lies outside of the tentacular ring. Most Bryozoans belong to this latter class.

CLASS ECTOPROCTA

FAMILY VESICULARIIDAE

Whorled Zoobotryon   *Zoobotryon verticillatum* (delle Chiaje)
    The transparent colonies form irregularly branching, often trifurcate and profuse masses of very soft and flaccid, algallike clusters on dock pilings and other shoreline structures. The species occurs from Bermuda to Brazil in our area. *(See drawing on page 70)*

Zoobotryon verticillatum
Whorled Zoobotryon *(see p. 69)*

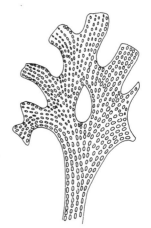

Membranipora tuberculata
Sargassum bryozoan

FAMILY MEMBRANIPORIDAE

Sargassum bryozoan   *Membranipora tuberculata* (Bosc)
    The colonies incrust algae, particularly *Sargassum* or Gulfweed, whose leaves, floats, and stems may be almost coated with a white, lacelike network. It is a circumtropical species and has been reported throughout the range covered by this book.

FAMILY BUGULIDAE

Common Bugula   *Bugula neritina* (Linnaeus)
    The colony is erect, bushy, forming reddish brown tufts up to 4 in. (10 cm) in height. This is a circumtropical species found throughout our region on mangrove roots and dock pilings.

Bugula neritina
Common Bugula

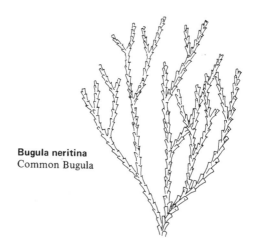

FAMILY SCHIZOPORELLIDAE

Single horn bryozoan   *Schizoporella unicornis* (Johnston)
    The colony is circular to irregular in outline and, depending upon the substrate, may be smooth, nodular, frilled or rising in irregular tubes. It may be transparent, colorless to yellow, orange, and deep purple. It is incrusting on shells, stones, algae, worm tubes, dock pilings, and boat bottoms.

FAMILY CHEILOPORINIDAE

Hooded bryozoan   *Watersipora cucullata* (Busk)
    The colonies are incrusting and are typically brownish purple to nearly black in color. They are common in south Florida on rocks and pilings and on boat bottoms. The color is distinctive.

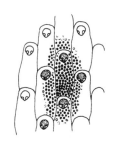

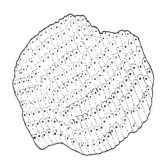

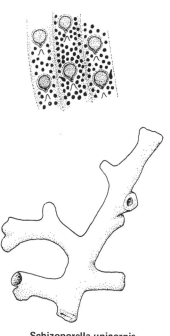

Schizoporella unicornis
Single horn bryozoan

Watersipora cucullata
Hooded bryozoan

Phylum Mollusca
Sea Slugs, Sea Hares, Nudibranchs, Octopus, and Squid

Mollusks are well known to most beach walkers from the numerous shells cast onto the beaches after storms. Despite their variation in design, mollusks belong to a well-defined group. They possess, with exceptions, an external shell, which may be coiled, tubular, bivalved, or formed of overlapping plates. Most also possess a rasping, tonguelike structure called a radula, a muscular foot, and a fleshy mantle, which, in addition to other functions, forms the shell.

The majority of species of these familiar animals are not discussed here because they are covered in detail by a profusion of easily obtainable books. Some mollusks, however, superficially appear so different from their familiar shelled relatives that they might not be recognized as mollusks by the novice. Those selected here do not bear an external calcareous shell. Most belong to the class Gastropoda, but four from the Cephalopoda are common in our shallow waters. The nudibranchs are among the most beautiful of marine invertebrates but are exceedingly difficult to collect. They seldom retain their shape in preservative and never their color; they must be seen alive to be enjoyed.

CLASS GASTROPODA
SUPERORDER OPISTHOBRANCHIA, ORDER SACOGLOSSA
FAMILY ELYSIIDAE

Common lettuce slug   *Tridachia crispata* (Mörch)
This is a common species in shallow water, particularly in sea grass beds. It attains a length of about 1-1/2 in. (38 mm). Its most conspicuous

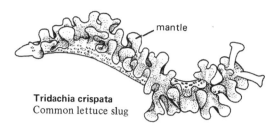

Tridachia crispata
Common lettuce slug

character is its frilled, undulating, and curled-up mantle. It is colored greenish or greenish blue flecked with white spots.

ORDER ANASPIDEA

FAMILY APLYSIIDAE
The Sea Hares or Inkfish

Spotted sea hare   *Aplysia dactylomela* Rang

The animal is roughly elliptical in shape with a flattened, crawling foot ventrally and two long flaps dorsally that cover a longitudinal central groove. The extensible head bears four fleshy flaps or tentacles. The internal shell is thin and leathery. The color is light tan or olive with dark streaks and rings. The animal is common in south Florida during the spring when it comes into very shallow water to deposit its tangled mass of egg strings. When disturbed it emits clouds of deep purple ink. It is worldwide in tropical and temperate seas.

Black sea hare   *Aplysia morio* (Verrill)

This sea hare attains a length of over 1 ft. (30 cm). It resembles the preceding species in general shape but has larger and more muscular dorsal flaps that it spreads like wings and swims vigorously. The internal shell is thin and leathery. The animal is very dark in color, nearly black, with golden brown flecks and streaks.

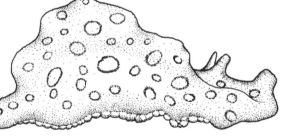

Aplysia dactylomela
Spotted sea hare
(after Pilsbry, 1895)

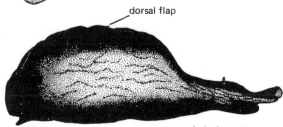

Aplysia morio
Black sea hare

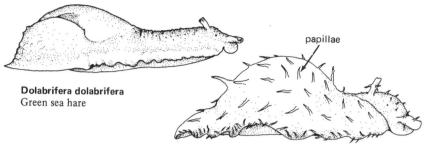

Dolabrifera dolabrifera
Green sea hare

papillae

Bursatella leachi plei
Ragged sea hare

Green sea hare   *Dolabrifera dolabrifera* (Rang)

The green sea hare has a compact, muscular body. The surface is roughened by low, oblong warts or papillae that densely cover the skin. The color is pale green to match the color of the seaweeds in which it lives. The internal shell is heavily calcified and covered by a brown periostracum (leathery layer). The species is found in most tropical and warm seas.

Ragged sea hare   *Bursatella leachi plei* (Rang)

The ragged sea hare has a more compact, rounded body than the others described, with distinct neck and head regions. The color is grayish white with blotches of dark brown. The body is covered with papillae of various sizes that give the animal a ragged or fringed appearance. Two long, fleshy tentacles or "ears" give the head a peculiarly mammalian appearance as it sways or bends to and fro in search of food. It has no internal shell. It attains a length of about 3 to 4 in. (7.5 to 10 cm).

ORDER NOTASPIDEA

FAMILY PLEUROBRANCHIDAE

Rough sea slug   *Pleurobranchus areolatus* Mörch

The animal is bluntly elliptical in outline, strongly flattened, and has a broad muscular foot. The body is dense, muscular, and contractile, and readily extrudes a thick mucus. Its background color is light golden brown flecked with grayish white, and it has scattered, circular, raised areas and low warts. It lives in coral rubble in shallow water.

ORDER DORIDOIDEA

FAMILY DORIDIDAE

Orange nudibranch   *Platydoris angustipes* (Mörch)

The body is strongly flattened, broadly elliptical in outline, and about 2 in. (5 cm) long. The upper surface is orange or orange red mottled and spotted with darker shades. The undersurface is paler. The gills in life are extended from an opening in the posterior section of the back. The animal has a somewhat hard, leathery consistency.

ORDER EOLIDOIDEA
FAMILY SCYLLAEIDAE

Sargassum nudibranch   *Scyllaea pelagica* Linnaeus

Although not strictly a seashore animal, the Sargassum nudibranch often comes ashore along with the sargassum weed upon which it lives. It is about 1 to 2 in. (25 to 50 mm) long, olive brown to orange brown, with flecks and spots of white, brown, and orange brown. It has about seven large lappets on the body which help it to match the sargassum weed.

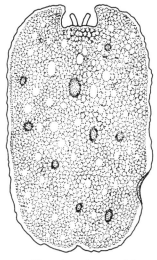

Pleurobranchus areolatus
Rough sea slug

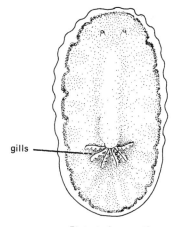

gills

Platydoris angustipes
Orange nudibranch

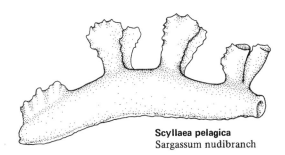

Scyllaea pelagica
Sargassum nudibranch

Class Cephalopoda

Octopus and Squid

The cephalopods are mollusks that have traded off the protection of a hard shell in favor of greater mobility and a high degree of intelligence. Numerous species occur in the West Indies, but only three octopus are fairly common and may be encountered in shallow water or cast upon the beach, excluding the papershell nautilus, which, because it has an external "shell," is not included here. Octopus live either in holes in the bottom or in empty mollusk shells, usually foraging at night for their prey — crustaceans and mollusks. Squid are open water animals not likely to be seen in shallow water except for the two noted here.

Order Octopoda

FAMILY OCTOPODIDAE

Common reef octopus   *Octopus briareus* Robson
This octopus lives on coral reefs and associated sea grass areas. It has an overall length of about 18 in. (46 cm). The side arms are conspicuously longer and fatter than the other arms. It is usually mottled and veined with bluish green or greenish blue on a whitish background.

Joubin's octopus   *Octopus joubini* Adam
The animal seldom attains a total length of more than 4 in. (10 cm). The arms are small and nearly equal in length. The color is dark brown to almost black. The females are often found in bivalve mollusk shells with

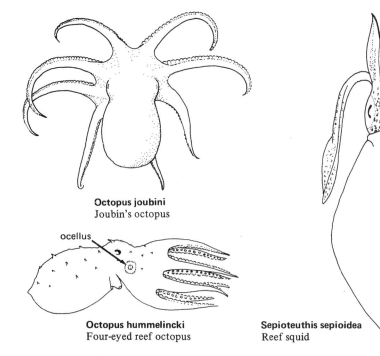

Octopus joubini
Joubin's octopus

Octopus hummelincki
Four-eyed reef octopus

Sepioteuthis sepioidea
Reef squid

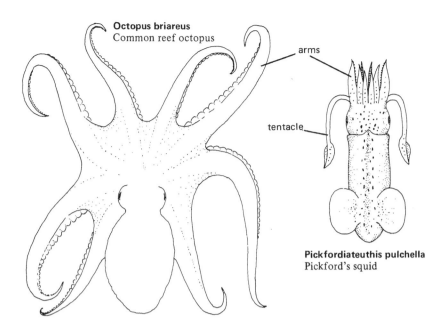

Octopus briareus
Common reef octopus

arms

tentacle

Pickfordiateuthis pulchella
Pickford's squid

their clutch of large eggs. They are often washed onto the beach. The species is known from south Florida to South America.

Four-eyed reef octopus   *Octopus hummelincki* Adam
  The four-eyed reef octopus is characterized by a dark spot beneath and in front of each eye. Within the dark spots is a deep blue ring or ocellus. The animal has numerous, low to high, straplike papillae scattered over the mantle, head, and arms. It may have a total length of about 8 in. (20 cm).

ORDER TEUTHOIDEA
FAMILY LOLIGINIDAE

Reef squid   *Sepioteuthis sepioidea* (Blainville)
  The mantle is somewhat cigar shaped and tubular, but it is bordered along nearly its entire length by long fins that give it an elliptical appearance. The animal is colored reddish brown with bars or spots of darker color in certain color phases. It may have a total length of about 10 in. (25 cm).

FAMILY PICKFORDIATEUTHIDAE

Pickford's squid   *Pickfordiateuthis pulchella* Voss
  This is the smallest species of squid in the Atlantic. It has a total length of slightly more than 1 in. (25 mm). The fins are circular and are near the posterior end of the mantle but are not united. It lives in sea grass beds.

Octopus, Squid / 77

Phylum Arthropoda
The Crustaceans

The arthropods include a vast array of animals very diverse in appearance, ranging from minute, planktonic, shrimplike animals to sessile barnacles and large crabs. All share in common an external hard shell and jointed legs. The phylum Arthropoda, both land and aquatic, contains an enormous number of species, all of which may never be described. In this book only the larger and more common species will be mentioned. Persons interested in learning more about these animals are advised to consult the pertinent books listed in the bibliography.

CLASS CRUSTACEA

This class contains those arthropods that breathe by means of gills or branchiae. These arthropods are segmented and have two pairs of antennae. Most segments have appendages that are divided into an inner and outer branch.

SUBCLASS CIRRIPEDIA
The Barnacles

The barnacles are shrimplike animals that are encased within a shell composed of few to numerous calcareous plates. The young are planktonic but soon settle onto suitable substrates, attach, and metamorphose into either a stalked or sessile animal protected by calcareous plates that may be closed to completely protect the animal within.

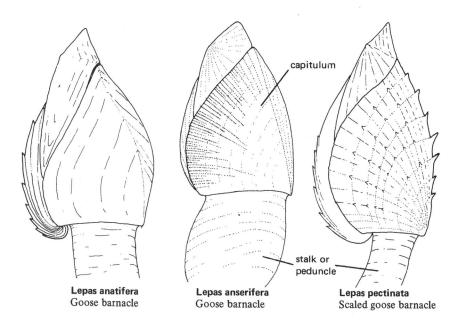

capitulum

stalk or
peduncle

Lepas anatifera
Goose barnacle

Lepas anserifera
Goose barnacle

Lepas pectinata
Scaled goose barnacle

ORDER THORACICA
True Barnacles
FAMILY LEPADIDAE

Goose barnacles   *Lepas anatifera* Linnaeus
                                    Lepas anserifera Linnaeus

Two species of large goose barnacles are commonly found attached to debris washed up on our beaches. Both have a long, fleshy stalk ending in a flat body formed of several connected calcareous plates. In *L. anatifera* the plates are nearly smooth and bluish white. The other species, *L. anserifera,* is whiter and the shell is radially grooved. Both are cosmopolitan in distribution. The common name is derived from the old myth that goose barnacles gave rise to geese.

Scaled goose barnacle   *Lepas pectinata* Spengler

This species is similar to the preceding one but is somewhat smaller and the valves or plates are ridged with scales or even spines that are conspicuous on the aperture edges. Minute specimens of *L. pectinata* are often found in the hollow of the last chamber of the ram's horn shell, *Spirula*. This species is cosmopolitan in warm seas.

FAMILY BALANIDAE

Ivory barnacle   *Balanus eburneus* Gould

The ivory barnacle is a sessile barnacle growing attached to rocks or wooden structures by means of a calcareous disc or plate that is fused to the side plates. It is conical or somewhat tubular with smooth walls. The plates are white, sometimes with a light yellow epidermis. It is found from the low water mark to about 20 fathoms (37 m). It is very similar to *B. improvisus,* also found in our range. There are several other species, all difficult to distinguish without dissection under the microscope.

Ribbed barnacle   *Tetraclita stalactifera* (Lamarck)

One of the most distinctive barnacles in the West Indian region, this species is conical to tubular in shape and covered with closely set, radial ribs. It is often eroded. It grows singly or in clumps in the intertidal zone above the zone inhabited by *Balanus*. It is dirty white, cream colored to grayish black. It, like *Balanus,* has a strong basal calcareous plate by which it fastens itself to intertidal rocks.

FAMILY CHTHAMALIDAE

Fragile barnacle   *Chthamalus fragilis* Darwin
Starred barnacle   *Chthamalus stellatus* (Poli)

There are two species of *Chthamalus* in the West Indian region — *C. stellatus* and *C. fragilis*. Both are small barnacles, living above the *Balanus* zone and more often found growing in protected regions. The shells are thin and the basal plate is not as heavy as in *Balanus* so that the shells are more easily removed from their attachment places. *C. stellatus* is often somewhat star-shaped while *C. fragilis* tends to be smoother and not as ridged. Both are whitish.

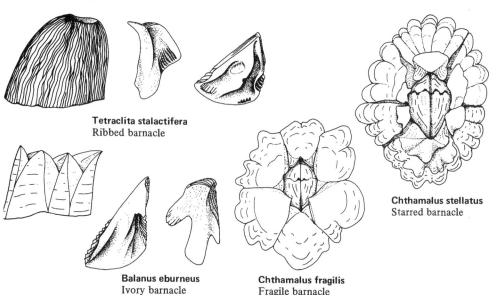

Tetraclita stalactifera
Ribbed barnacle

Chthamalus stellatus
Starred barnacle

Balanus eburneus
Ivory barnacle

Chthamalus fragilis
Fragile barnacle

SUBCLASS MALACOSTRACA

ORDER AMPHIPODA

The amphipods are elongate, laterally compressed, shrimplike animals, often somewhat strongly curved downward at each end. Most are small animals requiring the aide of a microscope for identification. They are included here only in order to mention the beach fleas or beach hoppers, the tiny hopping or jumping animals seen on the beach when seaweed is turned over or disturbed.

ORDER ISOPODA

The isopods are elongated crustaceans that are strongly dorsoventrally flattened. They form a diverse group, ranging from deepwater species more than 1 ft. (30 cm) long to microscopic mud dwellers. Many are parasitic and some are wood borers, which are seriously destructive animals to piers and other wooden seaside structures.

FAMILY LIMNORIIDAE

Three-spotted gribble   *Limnoria tripunctata* Menzies
    The animal is about 1/4 to 1/2 in. (6 to 13 mm) long, segmented, and with a large, somewhat rounded telson or tail fan that bears three distinct tubercles. The animal is oblong, rather broad, with short legs. When disturbed, it coils up like an armadillo. It bores into such wooden structures as old wharves and dock pilings and is extremely destructive.

FAMILY SPHAEROMIDAE

Mangrove gribble   *Sphaeroma tenebrans* Bate
    The mangrove gribble is smaller than *Limnoria*. It is short and broad with

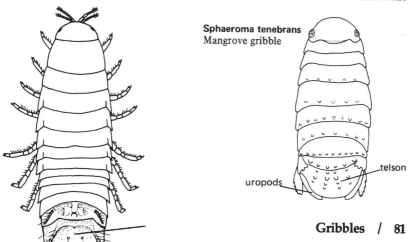

Sphaeroma tenebrans
Mangrove gribble

telson

uropods

Gribbles / 81

Limnoria tripunctata
Three-spotted gribble

a broad, shallow telson with narrow bladelike uropods, the outer one serrate. It bores into mangrove prop roots, causing extensive damage in some areas. It occurs from south Florida through the West Indies.

FAMILY LIGYDIDAE

The Boat or Dock Roaches

Sea roach or boat roach   *Ligia exotica* Roux

The boat roach is a little over 1 in. (25 mm) long, dark brown to almost black and ovoid, blunt anteriorly but tapering to a rather slender tail posteriorly. It is very loosely articulated. It has a pair of long antennae and two, long, branched uropods. It runs about swiftly over intertidal rocks, concrete sea walls, dock pilings, and small boats. A closely related species, *L. baudiniana* Milne Edwards, is lighter in color, more bluntly oval, and tightly compacted.

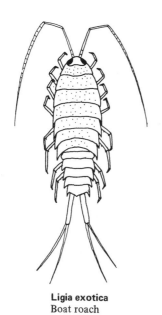

Ligia exotica
Boat roach

Ligia baudiniana
Boat roach

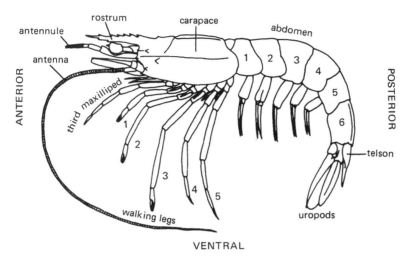

DORSAL

VENTRAL

Diagram of a penaeid shrimp
(after Voss, 1955)

ORDER DECAPODA

Shrimps, Lobsters, Crabs

These familiar crustaceans have a large chitinous carapace that covers the head and chest or thorax, and five pairs of legs or periopods, of which the first pair is composed of chelipeds. Claws or chelae are always found on the chelipeds and sometimes on the other legs, but when on the latter they are never enlarged.

SUBORDER NATANTIA

Shrimps

SECTION PENAEIDEA, FAMILY PENAEIDAE

Spotted or pink shrimp   *Penaeus duorarum* Burkenroad

The spotted, pink, or grooved shrimp can vary in color. Usually it is somewhat pinkish, but young specimens are whitish, grayish, pinkish, or greenish. Usually this species has a dark spot or splotch on each side of the tail. Full-grown adults may attain a total length of over 10 in. (25 cm) but are usually much smaller. This species has characteristic paired grooves running the length of the carapace on the median line. Three very similar species of grooved shrimp are found in our area: *P. duorarum,* the pink shrimp; *P. aztecus,* the brown shrimp; and *P. brasiliensis,* also called the pink spotted shrimp.

SECTION STENOPODIDEA

Stenopodid shrimp are easily recognized by the legs of the third pair of periopods, which are much larger than the other legs and bear large claws. Abdomen and carapace are usually spinous.

FAMILY STENOPODIDAE

Banded coral shrimp   *Stenopus hispidus* (Olivier)
   This beautiful little shrimp has a spiny abdomen, carapace, and third legs. Its ground color is transparent, white banded with purple bordered with orange red. Its long, slender antennae are waved slowly as a signal for fish to come to it in order to be cleaned of their parasites on which the shrimp feeds. It has a body length of about 2 in. (5 cm). It occurs throughout our range in coral reef habitats.

Golden coral shrimp   *Stenopus scutellatus* Rankin
   This species is similar to the preceding one except that the ground color is a pure yellow gold. Its abdomen and third legs are banded with bright orange red. It also is a cleaning shrimp. It occurs around coral reefs.

Scarlet stenopodid   *Microprosthema semilaeve* (von Martens)
   The scarlet stenopodid has a body length of less than 1 in. (25 mm). It has a broad, compact body and rather heavy third legs and claws. It has fewer spinelets than the preceding two species, hence its specific name, *semilaeve,* meaning "half or partly smooth." It is nearly solid bright scarlet with a few white bandings.

SECTION CARIDEA

The caridean shrimp are easily recognized because the plate or shell of the second abdominal segment overlaps both the preceding plate and the one behind. The abdomen also characteristically has a sharp downward bend and a dorsal hump.

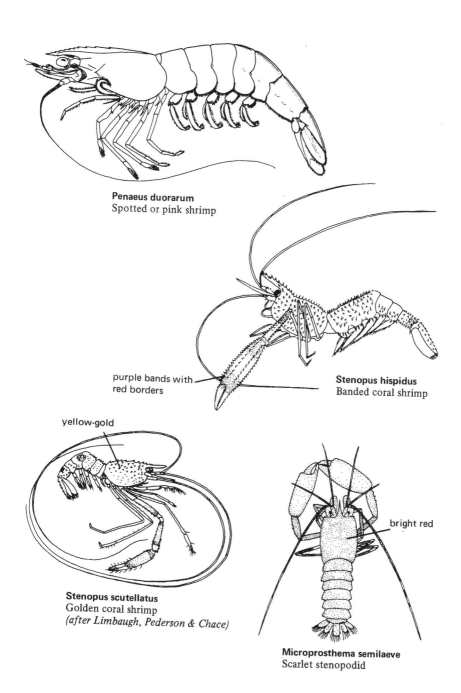

Penaeus duorarum
Spotted or pink shrimp

purple bands with
red borders

Stenopus hispidus
Banded coral shrimp

yellow-gold

Stenopus scutellatus
Golden coral shrimp
(after Limbaugh, Pederson & Chace)

bright red

Microprosthema semilaeve
Scarlet stenopodid

Shrimps / 85

FAMILY ALPHAEIDAE

The Snapping Shrimp

Banded snapping shrimp   *Alphaeus armillatus* Milne Edwards

The abdomen is banded alternately with white and greenish tan. The claws are greatly unequal, one being very heavy with short fingers; the other is slender with fingers better adapted for feeding. These shrimp make the sharp snapping sounds heard at night on boats moored to piers. The snapping sound is produced by a mechanism on the large claw. This shrimp lives in rocky and reef areas from Bermuda to Brazil.

Brown snapping shrimp   *Alphaeus armatus* Rathbun

This species is similar to the preceding one except that the body is brown with light tan flame markings on the side of the body. The antennae are banded red and white. The claws are mottled brown and tan.

Common snapping shrimp   *Synalpheus brevicarpus* (Herrick)

The genus *Synalpheus* contains a large number of closely related species that are very similar in appearance but in life may often be differentiated by color. The common snapping shrimp is greenish to greenish yellow with red splotching on the end of the large claw. It often lives along with other species in the galleries and holes in sponges, especially those of the loggerhead sponge, *Spheciospongia.*

FAMILY PALAEMONIDAE

Pederson's cleaning shrimp   *Periclimenes pedersoni* Chace
Ghost shrimp

This small shrimp has a nearly completely transparent body marked on the tail fan, abdominal hump, and legs with blotches of dark purple or lavender. It lives commensally with various sea anemones. It is a cleaning shrimp and lives in coral reef areas.

Spotted cleaning shrimp   *Periclimenes yucatanicus* (Ives)

The species is very similar to the preceding one but is beautifully marked with brown and eyelike spots and circles of white and dark brown. The legs and antennae are banded with white and dark brown or black. It barely attains 1 in. (25 mm) in length and is commensal with the larger shallow water sea anemones.

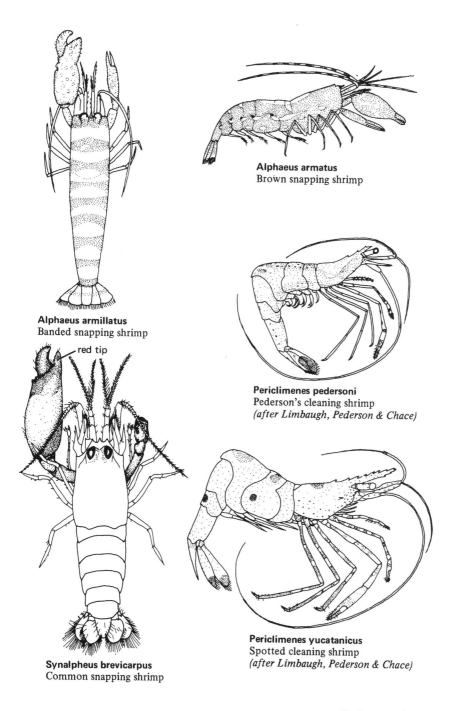

Alphaeus armatus
Brown snapping shrimp

Alphaeus armillatus
Banded snapping shrimp

red tip

Periclimenes pedersoni
Pederson's cleaning shrimp
(after Limbaugh, Pederson & Chace)

Synalpheus brevicarpus
Common snapping shrimp

Periclimenes yucatanicus
Spotted cleaning shrimp
(after Limbaugh, Pederson & Chace)

Two-clawed shrimp   *Brachycarpus biunguiculatus* (Lucas)
    The body is reddish brown with white bandings on the chelipeds. The large claw is long and cylindrical with short, somewhat slender dactyls. The last segment or dactyl of the last three pairs of walking legs are two-clawed or spined. The species is widely distributed in tropical seas.

FAMILY HIPPOLYTIDAE

Grass shrimp   *Tozeuma carolinensis* Kingsley
    The body is long and very slender with a prominent abdominal hump but without a sharp bend. The rostrum is long and nearly straight, very slender, with a series of teeth or spines on the ventral surface only. The shrimp is sometimes transparent but may be green when found in turtle grass or deep purple when living on purple alcyonarians, such as *Pseudopterogorgia acerosa.*

Scarlet-striped cleaning shrimp   *Lysmata grabhami* (Gordon)
Red-backed cleaning shrimp
    The colors are characteristic. The body is golden yellow with two broad bands of scarlet separated by a narrow white band on the back extending from the antennae to the tail fan. It occurs in shallow reef areas throughout our area.

Red-veined cleaning shrimp   *Lysmata wurdemanni* (Gibbes)
    This species is similar to the preceding one, but the body and appendages are pale pinkish white, veined with fine lines of bright reddish orange. It occurs in reef areas through the West Indies.

FAMILY GNATHOPHYLLIDAE

Bumblebee shrimp   *Gnathophyllum americanum* Guerin
    This is a small, stout, very compact-bodied shrimp with a cutoff look to the front. The entire body is covered with a series of broad bands of deep chocolate brown separated by narrow lines of yellow or gold. The legs are banded in white with chocolate and gold. The animal lives on sea urchins in grassy areas. It occurs from Bermuda to South America.

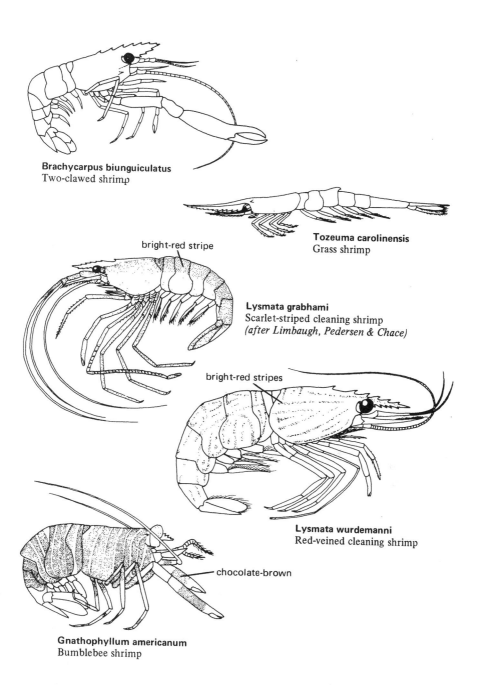

Brachycarpus biunguiculatus
Two-clawed shrimp

Tozeuma carolinensis
Grass shrimp

bright-red stripe

Lysmata grabhami
Scarlet-striped cleaning shrimp
(after Limbaugh, Pedersen & Chace)

bright-red stripes

Lysmata wurdemanni
Red-veined cleaning shrimp

chocolate-brown

Gnathophyllum americanum
Bumblebee shrimp

SUBORDER REPTANTIA, SECTION MACRURA
The Crawfish and Lobsters

FAMILY PALINURIDAE
Spiny Lobsters or Crawfish

Crawfish or spiny lobster   *Panulirus argus* (Latreille)

The common crawfish or spiny lobster attains an overall length of over 2 ft. (61 cm) and a weight of over 30 lb. (14 kilos). As a result of overfishing, few large specimens are seen today. This species is greenish, brownish blue to dark mahogany red with a few large yellowish spots on the tail and carapace. Very young specimens only 1 or 2 in. (25 to 50 mm) in length are found in grassy areas under rocks or sponges. As they grow larger they migrate into deeper water where they live in rocks, holes in coral reefs, and under large sponges. They are heavily fished wherever they occur, and most areas have closed seasons and limitations on collecting gear.

Spotted crawfish, Guinea lobster   *Panulirus guttatus* (Latreille)

This is similar to the preceding species except that the ground color is darker (dark green, purplish blue) and closely covered with white or cream spots over the carapace, tail, walking legs, and antennae. It is a smaller species, inhabiting rocky areas and coral reefs, and is nocturnal in its movements. It is less common than *P. argus* but has about the same range.

Smooth-tailed crawfish   *Panulirus laevicauda* (Latreille)

This species may be distinguished from the others by its more bluish green to purplish cast and the large white spots that are mainly found on the sides of the tail, not on the upper surface. This species is not common in the northern limit of its range.

FAMILY SCYLLARIDAE

Spanish or shovel-nosed lobster   *Scyllarides aequinoctialis* (Lund)

The animal has a broadly oval outline and short, stout legs and antennae. The carapace is heavy, thick, and covered with low nodules or rugosities. The tail is also broad and heavily armored. The antennules are broad, flat, and leaf shaped. The body and appendages are yellowish or reddish brown with brown splotches. There are four bright reddish purple spots on the first tail segment. It attains a length of over 12 in. (30 cm). This species is not numerous enough to be important commercially but is considered a delicacy by those fortunate enough to catch them.

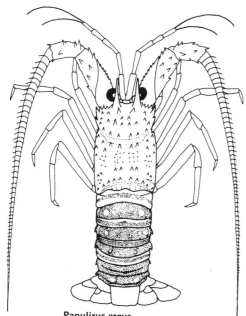

Panulirus argus
Crawfish, spiny lobster
(after Opresko et al., 1973)

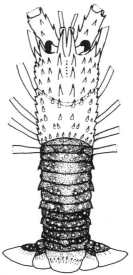

Panulirus guttatus
Spotted crawfish
(after Opresko et al., 1973)

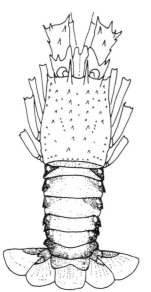

Panulirus laevicauda
Smooth-tailed crawfish
(after Opresko et al., 1973)

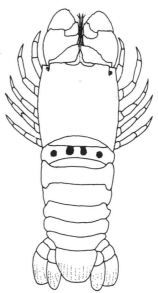

Scyllarides aequinoctialis
Spanish lobster

Crawfish and Lobsters / 91

Ridged slipper lobster, Slipper lobster   *Scyllarides nodifer* (Stimpson)

Similar to the preceding species, this lobster is smaller, about 5 in. (13 cm) long, and has a rougher shell. The color varies from yellowish to brownish, or dark gray. It lives in grassy and reef areas.

SECTION ANOMURA

SUPERFAMILY GALATHEIDEA, FAMILY PORCELLANIDAE

Poey's porcellanid   *Megalobrachium poeyi* (Guerin)

The crab is small, flattened, with a rounded carapace and enormous triangular claws with the hands deeply and strongly ridged. The animal is pubescent, especially on the claws where the hairs are long and coarse. It lives in shallow water on rocks or coral rubble.

Say's porcellanid   *Porcellana sayana* (Leach)

The animal is small with enormous chelipeds with sinuously curved claws. The carapace is flattened, somewhat circular, and minutely granular. The color is reddish with numerous pale to white spots over the entire upper surface. It occurs in rocky or coral rubble in shallow water and often lives with the hermit crab, *Petrochirus diogenes.*

SUPERFAMILY PAGURIDEA

The Hermit Crabs

FAMILY COENOBITIDAE

Land hermit crab   *Coenobita clypeatus* (Herbst)

This hermit crab is found along the seashore when young but goes further inland with maturity. It inhabits old mollusk shells and other hollow objects; one was even seen living in an old glass inkwell. The left cheliped is the larger and is covered with low, small, raised points. The left claw is blue to purple with orange dactyls. The dactyls of the walking legs are orange. The crab may have a carapace length of nearly 1-1/2 in. (38 mm).

FAMILY PAGURIDAE

Striped hermit crab   *Clibanarius vittatus* (Bosc)

A medium-sized crab, the chelipeds are equal in size, hairy, with short spines. It is greenish in color to dark brown with gray to white stripes, which are particularly noticeable on the legs.

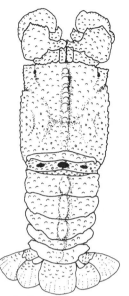

Scyllarides nodifer
Ridged slipper lobster

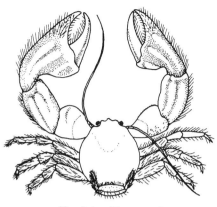

Megalobrachium poeyi
Poey's porcellanid
(after Schmitt, 1935)

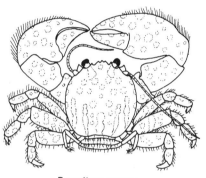

Porcellana sayana
Say's porcellanid
(after Williams, 1965)

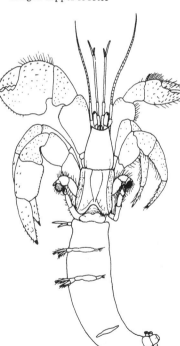

Coenobita clypeatus
Land hermit crab
(after Provenzano, 1959)

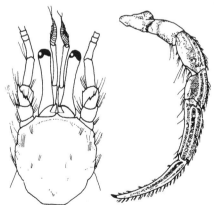

Clibanarius vittatus
Striped hermit crab
(after Provenzano, 1959)

Lobsters and Hermit Crabs / 93

Bar-eyed hermit crab *Dardanus fucosus* Biffar & Provenzano

This species is very similar to *D. venosus* (Milne Edwards). Both have hairy, spinous legs and chelae, cream colored, barred with orange bands. *Dardanus fucosus* has a black bar across the eyes while *D. venosus* is whitish to bluish.

Giant hermit crab *Petrochirus diogenes* Linnaeus

This is the largest hermit crab in the West Indies and may reach a total length of over 1 ft. (30 cm). The chelipeds are massive, the right slightly larger, and rough, the surface appearing as if covered with sharp, overlapping, irregular scales. The color is reddish with bandings of red and white on the antennae, their peduncles longitudinally striped with red and white. This crab often occupies the shell of the pink conch.

Long-armed hermit crab *Pagurus longicarpus* Say

A small hermit crab with the right cheliped much longer and larger than the left. The claw is comparatively long and slender. The color is very variable, often greenish gray to brown.

Thumb-clawed hermit crab *Pagurus pollicaris* Say

The right claw is distinctly the larger, flattened and semicircular. The outer margin is sharply toothed while the middle of the hand has three longitudinal rows of low spinules. The characteristic feature is the free finger or "thumb," which has a strong angle on its outer margin. The color is grayish tan with white chelipeds with gray margins.

SUPERFAMILY HIPPIDEA, FAMILY HIPPIDAE

Sand Fleas or Mole Crabs

Common sand flea *Emerita talpoida* Say

The sand flea is oval in total body shape, both the abdomen and the legs held tightly clasped beneath the oval carapace. The second antennae are large and plumose for straining detritus from seawater. The body is about 1 to 1-1/2 in. (25 to 38 mm) long and has an overall sandy yellow color. The sand flea burrows just below the surface of the sand on wave-swept beaches throughout our range.

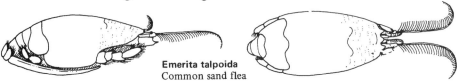

Emerita talpoida
Common sand flea

The ringed anemone *Bartholomea annulata (see page 46)* is fastened to old coral covered by an incrusting coralline alga. The rough file shell *Lima scabra* with bright red mantle and tentacles is in the foreground. To the far right are the black spines of the long-spined urchin *Diadema antillarum (see page 136)*. (Photo: Dr. William J. Jahoda)

A blue button *Porpita linneana (see page 34)*, its delicate disc fringed by blue tentacles, is being fed upon by a pelagic mollusk *Glaucus marinus*. (Photo: William M. Stephens)

The horned feather worm *Spirobranchus giganteus (see page 66)* expands its double crown from a calcareous tube in a coral head. The two purple forks of the horn or operculum show just below the featherlike branchiae. (Photo: Dr. William J. Jahoda)

Dangerous, needle-sharp poisonous spines of the long-spined sea urchin *Diadema antillarum (see page 136)* often penetrate hands and feet of unwary waders and swimmers. (Photo: Dr. Ronald F. Thomas)

Like a mass of frills, the common lettuce slug *Tridachia crispata (see page 72)* is often seen crawling about on sea grasses or corals. (Photo: Carl Roessler)

Holding his large claw menacingly before him, a great land crab *Cardisoma guanhumi (see page 112)*, eyes erect, watches the intruding photographer. (Photo: John B. Shoup)

The arrow crab *Stenorhynchus seticornis (see page 116)* prowls a rock patch on delicate stiltlike legs. This graceful crab is a favorite with marine aquarists. (Photo: Dr. Dennis M. Opresko)

A box crab *Calappa (see page 98)* stares at an intruder as it burrows into the sand. (Photo: Dr. Ronald F. Thomas)

Eyes bulging, the mangrove crab *Aratus pisonii (see page 110)* pauses in flight on a mangrove limb. (Photo: Dr. Lowell Thomas)

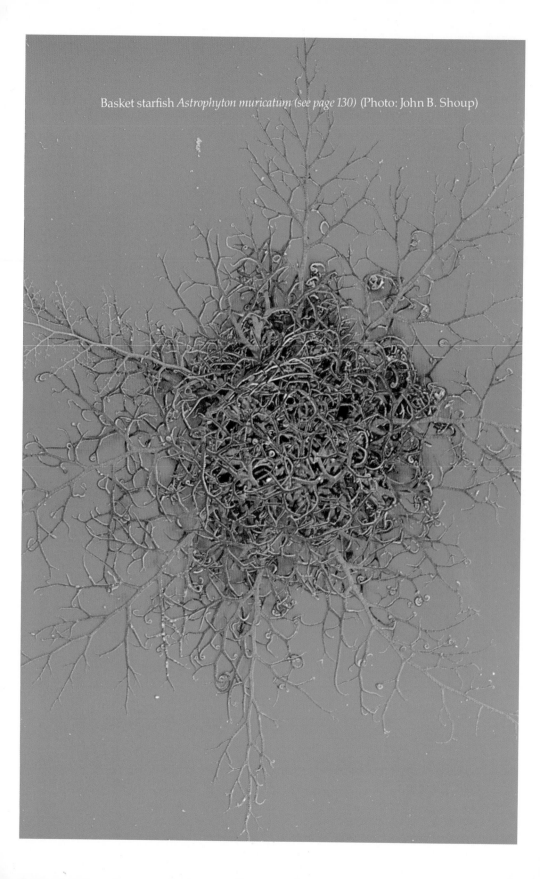

Basket starfish *Astrophyton muricatum (see page 130)* (Photo: John B. Shoup)

Reef octopus *Octopus briareus (see page 77)* (Photo: Roger T. Hanlon)

Above right: The rock-boring urchin *Echinometra lucunter (see page 138)* is usually found in holes in coral rock just below the low tide mark. (Photo: Dr. Ronald F. Thomas)
Above left: The green rock-boring urchin *Echinometra viridis (see page 138)* occupies a niche similar to the rock-boring urchin. Note the light rings around the base of the spines. (Photo: Dr. Ronald F. Thomas)

Below: The variegated urchin *Lytechinus variegatus (see page 137)* lives on open sea grass beds, often camouflaged with bits of shell and grass leaves. (Photo: Dr. Ronald F. Thomas)

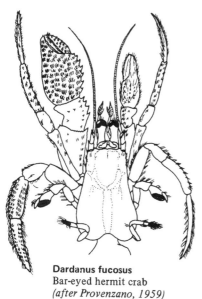

Dardanus fucosus
Bar-eyed hermit crab
(after Provenzano, 1959)

Petrochirus diogenes
Giant hermit crab
(after Provenzano, 1959)

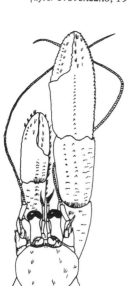

Pagurus longicarpus
Long-armed hermit crab
(after Provenzano, 1959)

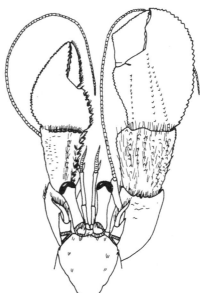

Pagurus pollicaris
Thumb-clawed hermit crab
(after Provenzano, 1959)

Hermit Crabs and Sand Fleas / 95

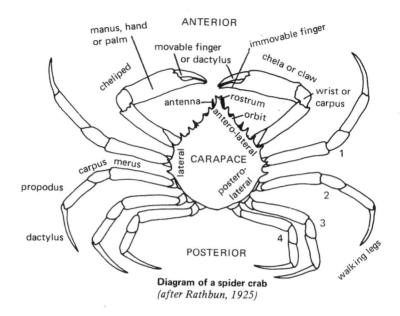

Diagram of a spider crab
(after Rathbun, 1925)

SECTION BRACHYURA

The True Crabs

The true crabs are familiar animals to everyone who visits the seashore. They are found from dry land to considerable depths. They range in size from almost microscopic to giants 6 ft. (2 m) or more across the out-stretched arms. Most species are of no economic importance, but some, like the blue crab and the stone crab, are highly prized gastronomic delights.

The carapace or shell is most often short and broad, usually bearing spines, and the abdomen is small and strongly flexed under the shell. There are three subsections: Dromiacea, Oxystomata, and Brachygnatha.

SUBSECTION DROMIACEA

The carapace or shell is longer than wide, the abdomen is not so greatly reduced, and the last two pairs of legs are reduced in size; the last pair is dorsal.

FAMILY DROMIIDAE

Sponge crab   *Dromia erythropus* (Edwards)

The carapace of this crab is slightly wider than long and is densely covered with stiff, dark brown or blackish hairs. The carapace is whitish;

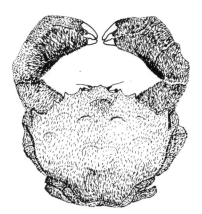

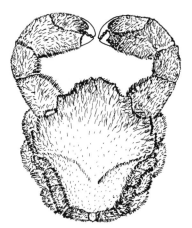

Dromia erythropus
Sponge crab
(after Rathbun, 1937)

Dromidia antillensis
Lesser sponge crab
(after Rathbun, 1937)

the tips of the legs are naked and colored light red. The crab usually covers itself with a piece of live sponge hollowed out to fit the curve of its carapace. It holds this on its back with the sharp curved dactylus of the last pair of legs, which are above the carapace. It attains a size of about 4 to 5 in. (10 to 13 cm) carapace width.

Lesser sponge crab   *Dromidia antillensis* Stimpson

The carapace is convex and covered with hairs. It is longer than wide with the lateral margins parallel or nearly so. The legs of the last pair are longer than those of the preceding pair. This crab carries a large covering on its back, usually a sponge but often an ascidian colony or a zoanthid. The color is brownish red to yellowish green, and the tips of the claws are crimson.

SUBSECTION OXYSTOMATA

The carapace is somewhat circular. The mouth field is triangular with the apex pointed forward. The posterior legs are somewhat reduced.

FAMILY LEUCOSIIDAE

Purse crab   *Persephone punctata* (Linnaeus)

The purse crab, and its close relatives, has a nearly round or oval, strongly arched carapace covered with small granules. The margin of the anterior half projects between the eyes and has a small spine on each side posterior to the eye. The posterior border of the shell has three spines, a strong central one and a smaller one on each side. The chelipeds are long, moderately stout, with short fingers. The crab is grayish or bluish, often with several large russet or red spots. It lives on sandy bottom from the West Indies to Brazil. Two similar forms, *P. punctata aequilonaris* and *P. crinita* also occur in Florida.

Stimpson's Iliacantha   *Iliacantha subglobosa* Stimpson
    This is similar to the preceding species but rounder, with no teeth on the anterior half of the carapace and with larger and more numerous granules. The marginal posterior teeth are blunter, but the median tooth is longer and sharper. The legs and chelipeds are much more slender, and the tingers of the claws are longer than the palm. A close relative with longer, sharper posterior spines, *I. liodactylus*, occurs from the west coast of Florida throughout the West Indies.

FAMILY CALAPPIDAE

Flamed box crab   *Calappa flammea* (Herbst)
    The carapace is hemispherical, rounded in front, almost straight behind. The posterior margins form a thin roof over the legs, partially hiding them. The large claws are flattened, triangular, with a crest above, and the dactyls or fingers strongly bent downward. The color is grayish with flame markings of purplish brown on the shell and bandings on the legs. The claw has several spots of purple and orange. This is a common, sand-dwelling crab found from the intertidal zone to moderate depths.

Yellow box crab   *Calappa gallus* (Herbst)
    Similar to the preceding species but with the surface of the shell rough, covered with nodules and ridges, this crab is orange to orange brown, yellow beneath. The front of the carapace and the upper parts of the claws are covered with dark red or reddish brown spots. The legs are yellow with fine red lines. It lives on sandy bottom.

Calico crab, Dolly Varden crab   *Hepatus epheliticus* (Linnaeus)
    The carapace has a rounded contour with very small, blunt teeth. The claws are flattened and have several longitudinal ridges. The shell is yellowish white or brownish with irregular spots of dark red, each lined by a darker ring. In some large adults only the rings are present. This crab is found on sandy bottom in shallow water.

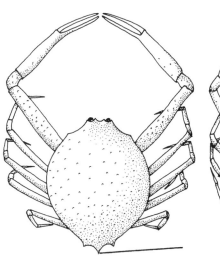

Persephone punctata
Purse crab
(after Rathbun, 1937)

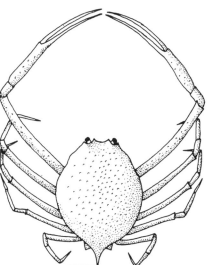

Iliacantha subglobosa
Stimpson's Iliacantha
(after Rathbun, 1937)

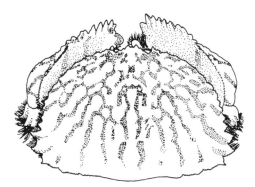

Calappa flammea
Flamed box crab
(after Rathbun, 1937)

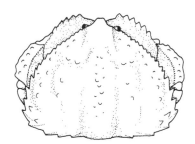

Calappa gallus
Yellow box crab
(after Rathbun, 1937)

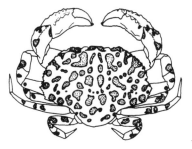

Hepatus epheliticus
Calico crab
(after Williams, 1965)

SUBSECTION BRACHYGNATHA
SUPERFAMILY BRACHYRHYNCHA
The Cancroid Crabs

The carapace is oval to circular and bears spines on the anterior and lateral borders. The mouth frame is square and covered by the shieldlike third maxillipeds.

FAMILY PORTUNIDAE

Sargassum crab, Say's Portunus   *Portunus sayi* (Gibbes)
The carapace is highly arched, very smooth and almost glossy. It has a width of about 2 in. (5 cm). The palms of the claws bear two spines, one at each end. The last pair of legs bears a paddle-shaped appendage used for swimming. The color is mottled olive green or purplish, variegated with yellowish brown and with white spots. The color pattern mimics the color of sargassum weed, which it lives among in midocean and along the course of the Gulf Stream.

Spiny-handed Portunus   *Portunus spinimanus* Latreille
A larger crab than the preceding one, it has about eight nearly equal spines on the lateral margins of the carapace, the one at the posterior angle little larger than the others in adults. The carapace is covered with short, thick hairs. The hand of the claw has two spines and a tuberculate longitudinal ridge on the outer upper surface. The carapace attains a width of about 3 in. (7.5 cm). The hairs are yellowish; there are reddish ridges on the carapace. The lateral teeth are reddish at the base, whitish at the tips. The claw fingers are whitish with red tips. This species lives on sandy bottom in shallow water.

Blue crab, common edible crab   *Callinectes sapidus* Rathbun
This is the common edible blue crab of the Atlantic coast. It is best distinguished from its many relatives by its larger size when adult and the lateral teeth, which are somewhat narrow at their bases but sharply and acutely pointed. There are two median teeth between the orbits. As in *Portunus*, there is a paddle-shaped appendage on the last legs. It lives on muddy bottom in shallow water and attains a width across the carapace of 6 to 8 in. (15 to 20 cm). The color is grayish or bluish green with bright red on the spines. A subspecies, *C. sapidus acutidens*, occurs only in the tropical part of the range. It has sharper lateral teeth and four small teeth between the orbits. It is somewhat smaller.

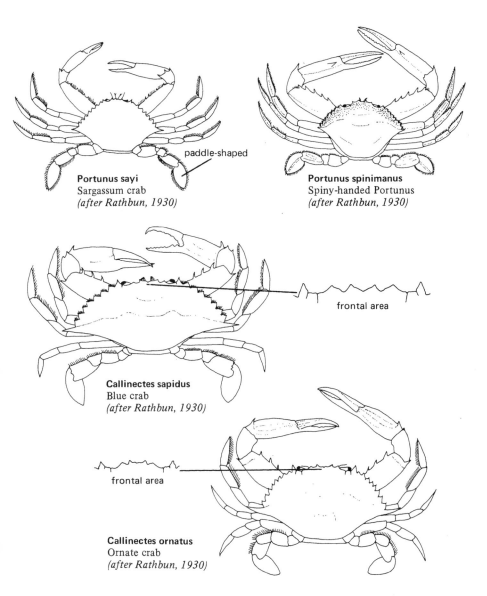

Portunus sayi
Sargassum crab
(after Rathbun, 1930)

paddle-shaped

Portunus spinimanus
Spiny-handed Portunus
(after Rathbun, 1930)

Callinectes sapidus
Blue crab
(after Rathbun, 1930)

frontal area

frontal area

Callinectes ornatus
Ornate crab
(after Rathbun, 1930)

Ornate crab   *Callinectes ornatus* Ordway

The ornate crab is very similar to the blue crab except that the lateral teeth are very broad and shallow. It attains a width of about 4 to 5 in. (10 to 13 cm). It derives its name from its ornate colors. The carapace is greenish with brownish hairs. The teeth are yellowish with white tips. The walking legs are bright blue with coral red tips. These crabs live on muddy and sandy bottom.

Marginal crab   *Callinectes marginatus* (Milne-Edwards)

Similar to the preceding species except that the lateral spines are some-what more distinctly set apart, the carapace is speckled with coarse granules and the lateral spine is short. It attains a width of about 4 in. (10 cm). It is dull brown with bluish black areas. The claw is brown above but bluish black on the inner surface. It inhabits shallow, muddy bottoms.

Forceps crab   *Lupella forceps* (Fabricius)

This is one of the most characteristic crabs of the West Indian Province. It is easily recognized by the very prominent and projecting posterolateral tooth of the carapace, the long, slender walking legs, and, in the male, the extremely long and slender fingers of the claws, from which it gets its name. It reaches a width of about 3 in. (7.5 cm) across the carapace. It occurs in shallow to moderate depths.

Speckled crab   *Arenaeus cribrarius* (Lamarck)

The upper surface of the carapace is light brownish covered with closely set, small, white or light yellow spots. The same pattern is found on the claws except that the spots are somewhat larger. There is a single spine at the outer end of the palm. The carapace width is about 5 in. (13 cm).

Red crab   *Cronius ruber* (Lamarck)

The carapace is hexagonal, smooth, and covered with short hairs. The posterolateral tooth is scarcely larger than the preceding teeth. The crab is violet red or deep purplish red, marbled with a lighter shade or with white. The tips of all the spines are black. It inhabits shallow water but is more common in somewhat deeper water.

FAMILY XANTHIDAE

Coral crab, queen crab   *Carpilius corallinus* (Herbst)

This is one of the most beautiful crabs in our area. The carapace is smooth and heavy with no teeth except for a blunt one at the posterolateral corner. The ground color is pale to brick red with scarlet spots with meandering lines and spots of white and yellow. The ends of the fingers of the claws are brown. This is one of the largest West Indian crabs, attaining a carapace width of 6 in. (15 cm) and considerable weight. It is highly prized as food. It occurs among coral reefs and rocky rubble in shallow water.

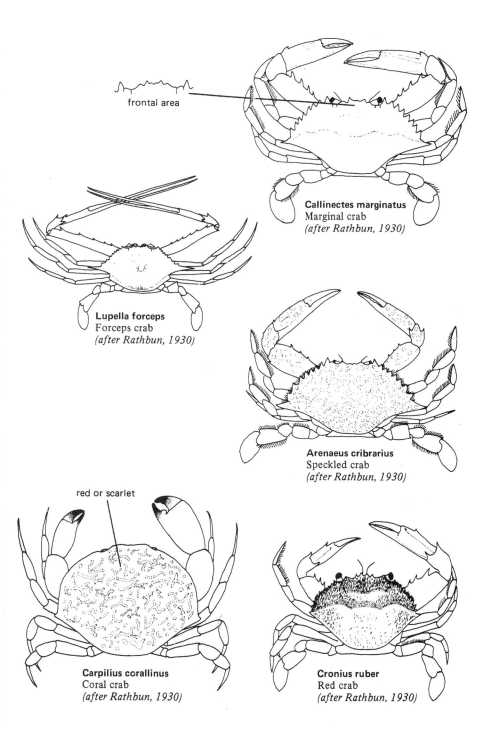

frontal area

Callinectes marginatus
Marginal crab
(after Rathbun, 1930)

Lupella forceps
Forceps crab
(after Rathbun, 1930)

Arenaeus cribrarius
Speckled crab
(after Rathbun, 1930)

red or scarlet

Carpilius corallinus
Coral crab
(after Rathbun, 1930)

Cronius ruber
Red crab
(after Rathbun, 1930)

Herbst's Platypodia   *Platypodia spectabilis* (Herbst)
The carapace is scarcely 1 in. (2.5 cm) across, elliptical, with rounded, almost smooth lobules on the upper surface. The hand is short with a smooth dorsal crest and a series of granular lines on the outer surface. The color is chocolate brown with some yellow spots bordered with black and blue. The legs are red with tricolored stripes of yellow, black, and blue. It occurs on coral reefs and rubble.

Hairy Actaea   *Actaea setigera* (Milne-Edwards)
The carapace is elliptical in front, the upper surface divided into distinct lobes. Almost the entire surface of the animal, including the legs and claws, is covered with short, stiff hairs. The color is light orange red with yellow bristles and whitish granules, and the fingers of the claws are black or dark purplish brown. This crab lives on reefs and surrounding areas.

Spiny Actaea   *Actaea acantha* (Milne-Edwards)
This is similar to the preceding species except that beneath the long hairs on the carapace are numerous sharp spines or tubercles; the surface is divided by deep grooves. The animal may attain a width of slightly more than 1 in. (2.5 cm). Its color is purplish with brown claws. It lives in coral reefs and rubble.

Eroded reef crab   *Glyptoxanthus erosus* (Stimpson)
This unusual little crab has a thick carapace and body which have the appearance of being eroded away, leaving a surface series of meandering ridges and spots. The body has a creamy color, lighter on the ridges and somewhat darker in the pits, with small spots of bright red. The tips of the legs are reddish with yellowish beyond. The carapace may have a width of slightly more than 2 in. (5 cm). This crab lives on reefs and rocky bottoms, often being found in holes in which they seem to be imprisoned.

Florida Leptodius   *Leptodius floridanus* (Gibbes)
This genus has a number of very similar species that are difficult to distinguish except by a specialist. This species has a smooth, lobulate carapace bordered by sharp teeth. The legs are short and the claws are stout. The ground color is ivory white, becoming darker anteriorly on the carapace with irregular dark spots. The upper portions of the claws are dark green, fading to almost white beneath. Both fingers are dark brown or chestnut ribbed with white. The dark color of the immovable finger extends back onto the palm. This crab, rarely exceeding 1 in. (2.5 cm) in width, is found on reefs.

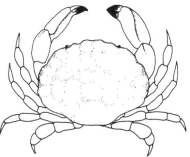

Platypodia spectabilis
Herbst's Platypodia
(after Rathbun, 1930)

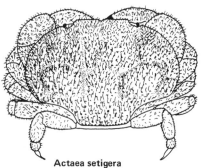

Actaea setigera
Hairy Actaea
(after Rathbun, 1930)

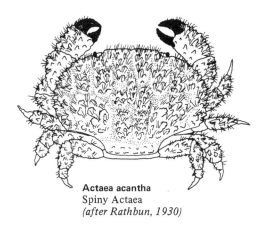

Actaea acantha
Spiny Actaea
(after Rathbun, 1930)

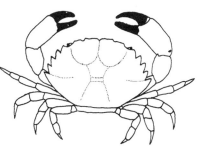

Glyptoxanthus erosus
Eroded reef crab
(after Rathbun, 1930)

Leptodius floridanus
Florida Leptodius
(after Rathbun, 1930)

Crabs / 105

Herbst's Panopeus   *Panopeus herbsti* Milne Edwards

There are a number of small, difficult to identify species in this genus in our area. This species has a hexagonal carapace that is slightly granular with prominent, widely spaced teeth. The legs are hairy and slender; the claws are massive. The carapace is dull brownish green, paler below, with claws deeper colored and sometimes spotted with claret brown. The fingers are blackish with the dark color on the immovable finger extending back onto the palm. This is a variable species with a number of named forms. It lives in shallow water and is commonly found in oyster beds, mangrove roots, and other secluded habitats.

Stone crab   *Menippe mercenaria* (Say)

This well-known, edible crab is easily recognized by its heavy, smooth carapace bordered by flat lobes rather than spines, and its massive claws. There is a patch of ridges on the inside of the palm which, when rubbed against the edge of the carapace, gives off the typical sound produced by this crab. The young are a dark bluish purple with a white spot on the wrist. Adults are dark brownish red, mottled and speckled with dusky gray. The fingers of the claws are black; the black on the immovable finger does not extend back onto the palm. Adults attain a carapace width of about 5 in. (13 cm). The young live in shoreline rubble, old oyster shells, and on pilings. Adults move out to shallow water and normally live in burrows. In the stone crab fishery only the claws are harvested; the crabs soon grow new ones.

Say's Pilumnus   *Pilumnus sayi* Rathbun

There are numerous species of this genus in our area. This species is hairy, but the hairs do not conceal the carapace below. These sparse, thin, short, downy hairs are interspersed with many long, stout hairs with pointed tips. There are four, occasionally three, anterolateral spines. The palms of the claws are hairy or partly so but smooth or nearly so on the outer surface. The adults have a width of about 1 in. (2.5 cm). The color is grayish brown, irregularly suffused with red. The spines are black, the hairs yellow. This crab is common on shelly bottoms and wharf pilings.

Horned crab   *Heteractaea ceratopus* (Stimpson)

The carapace is covered with nodules and spines interspersed with tufts of short hair. There is a long, curved spine or horn on the carpus of each walking leg. The claws are nodular and spinous. The color is milk white, with the naked parts of the palms bright red or purple, the fingers black. The hairs are russet. This crab reaches a width of slightly more than 1 in. (2.5 m).

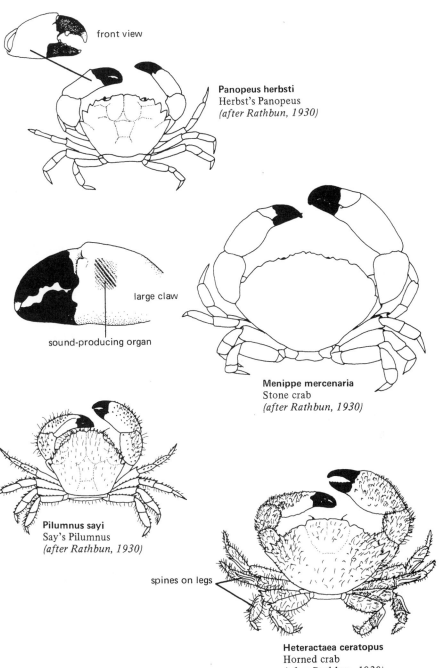

front view

Panopeus herbsti
Herbst's Panopeus
(after Rathbun, 1930)

large claw

sound-producing organ

Menippe mercenaria
Stone crab
(after Rathbun, 1930)

Pilumnus sayi
Say's Pilumnus
(after Rathbun, 1930)

spines on legs

Heteractaea ceratopus
Horned crab
(after Rathbun, 1930)

Crabs / 107

Calico crab   *Eriphia gonagra* (Fabricius)
This small crab is immediately identifiable by the large, round, flattened tubercles on the anterior part of the carapace and especially on the hands of the claws. The carapace is brownish green. The ground color of the claws is light bluish purple, and the fingers and tubercles are deep purplish brown. The carapace may have a width of nearly 2 in. (5 cm). This crab lives among rocks, reefs, and rubble.

The Grapsoid Crabs

The grapsoid crabs in general have squarish carapaces, usually with no spines or with insignificant ones, and the frontal area of the carapace is bent downward.

FAMILY GRAPSIDAE

Sally Lightfoot   *Grapsus grapsus* (Linnaeus)
This is the swiftest and nimblest of all crabs. Its squarish body is variegated with deep red and light green or is entirely dark red. The running legs are broad and flattened. The claws are small and bright red. This animal lives on intertidal rocks where it dashes about between the waves, spending much time in the air. It attains a carapace width of about 3 in. (7.5 cm). They are exceedingly difficult to catch.

Mangrove or tree crab   *Goniopsis cruentata* (Latreille)
The carapace is quadrate with a single spine on each side. Both the carapace and the legs are crossed by fine lines of tubercles. The merus of the chelipeds is expanded into a thin sheet with coarse spines. The color is brownish yellow or brick red with red legs with spots of darker red. The claws are red except for the palms. The tips of all the legs are yellowish. This species inhabits mangrove swamps where it lives on the roots and trunks of the trees or on wet, muddy shores.

Gibbes' Pachygrapsus   *Pachygrapsus transversus* (Gibbes)
The sides of the carapace converge posteriorly. The surface of the carapace is covered with transverse and oblique lines of fine tubercles. The front between the orbits is slightly sinuous. The upper surface of the movable finger of the claw is smooth. The color is brownish to slightly pinkish. The carapace has a width of about 1 in. (2.5 cm) or less. This species is found among stones, mangrove roots, and on sandy shores.

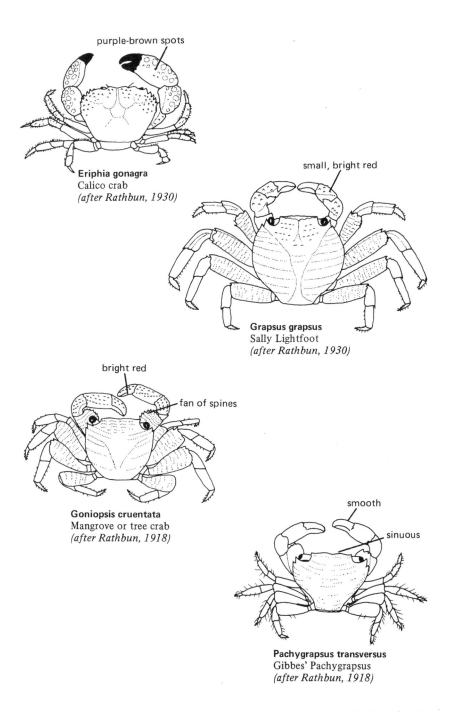

purple-brown spots

Eriphia gonagra
Calico crab
(after Rathbun, 1930)

small, bright red

Grapsus grapsus
Sally Lightfoot
(after Rathbun, 1930)

bright red

fan of spines

Goniopsis cruentata
Mangrove or tree crab
(after Rathbun, 1918)

smooth

sinuous

Pachygrapsus transversus
Gibbes' Pachygrapsus
(after Rathbun, 1918)

Wharf crab   *Pachygrapsus gracilis* (Saussure)
    Although very similar to the preceding species, this crab may be differentiated from it by the convex frontal area between the orbits, the tuberculations on the upper edge of the movable finger of the claw, and the pinkish coloration. It is commonly found above the water surface on pilings, wharves, and other structures.

Gulf weed crab   *Planes minutus* (Linnaeus)
    This little crab is pelagic, living on *Sargassum* and other floating material. It has a convex carapace with strongly curved sides; short, stout legs; and small, equal-sized claws. In color it mimics sargassum weed, being mottled with light greenish yellow or yellow on an olive green background. It occurs on gulfweed in all tropical and temperate seas.

Mangrove crab   *Sesarma curacaoense* de Man
    This is a small crab less than 1/2 in. (13 mm) wide. The carapace is square, almost smooth, with a lateral tooth behind the orbital tooth. There are spots of lighter color on the anterior half of the carapace. It lives among leaves and mangrove roots.

Wood crab, friendly crab   *Sesarma cinereum* (Bosc)
    Similar to the preceding species, this one differs from it in that a spine is not present behind the orbital spine. The carapace is nearly smooth. The merus of the third walking leg is about 2.5 times as long as wide. This crab lives along the water's edge under logs, in drift and pilings, and is frequently found on boats.

Beach crab   *Sesarma ricordi* Milne Edwards
    This species is similar to the preceding species, but the carapace and chelipeds are covered with granules. The merus of the third walking legs is three times as long as wide. This crab is colored orange or reddish yellow, finely speckled by the black hairs of the carapace. It has considerable variation, however, and may be almost solid brown. It lives on driftwood, rocks, pilings, and old seaweed.

Mangrove crab, tree crab   *Aratus pisonii* (Milne Edwards)
    The carapace is turned strongly inward posteriorly, smooth to the naked eye, but finely granulated anteriorly. There are no lateral spines behind the orbital spine. The legs, and particularly the claws, are granulose. There is a patch of conspicuous hairs on the outer surface of the claws. This species attains a width of just under 1 in. (2.5 cm). It is usually a mottled green with reddish legs but is highly variable in color. It lives on mangroves and on rocks, pilings, and other structures near the shore.

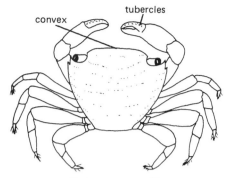

Pachygrapsus gracilis
Wharf crab
(after Rathbun, 1918)

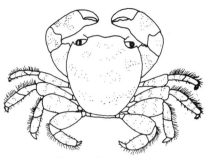

Planes minutus
Gulf weed crab
(after Rathbun, 1918)

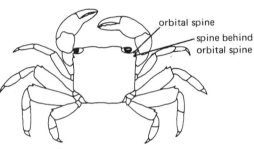

Sesarma curacaoense
Mangrove crab
(after Rathbun, 1918)

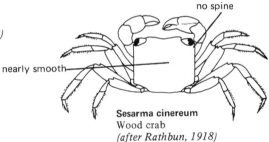

Sesarma cinereum
Wood crab
(after Rathbun, 1918)

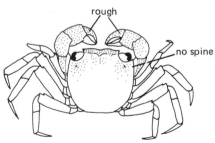

Sesarma ricordi
Beach crab
(after Rathbun, 1918)

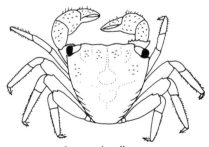

Aratus pisonii
Mangrove crab
(after Rathbun, 1918)

Crabs / 111

Flattened Plagusia   *Plagusia depressa* (Fabricius)
   The nearly circular carapace is tuberculate, the tubercles fringed with hairs. There are four widely spaced anterolateral teeth. The claws are massive and covered with longitudinal rows of tubercles. The color of the carapace is light reddish dotted with dark red; the hairs around the tubercles are blackish. The underside is yellow. The carapace may be nearly 2 in. (5 cm) wide. This crab lives on rocks or rocky shores or on coral reefs.

Spray crab   *Percnon gibbesi* (Milne Edwards)
   The carapace is ovate, very thin, and disclike. The upper surface is covered with a few low, flattened tubercles and little short bristles. The legs are long and slender, strongly flattened, with a row of sharp spines along the anterior edge of the merus. The claws are short and swollen. The color is variegated brown, flesh color, and pinkish on the carapace, with a median stripe of pale blue. The legs are banded with reddish brown and light pink. This crab lives on reefs and on exposed rocks in the spray and splash zone.

FAMILY GECARCINIDAE

The Land Crabs

Great land crab   *Cardisoma guanhumi* Latreille
   This is our largest land crab, living in deep holes in sand or mud areas. It is highly prized as food in the Bahamas and West Indies. The carapace is smooth except for a fine line or ridge along the sides. The legs are long and only slightly hairy. The chelipeds of the male are large and one is gigantic. The carapace may have a width of nearly 5 in. (13 cm), but the spread across the claws may be more than 2 ft. (61 cm). The adult coloration is bluish, tinged ashy gray or dirty white; the young are violet.

Hairy land crab   *Ucides cordatus* (Linnaeus)
   This crab is almost as large as the preceding one, but it may be immediately separated by the transversely oval carapace. The legs are long and sparsely to heavily covered with soft hairs. The claws are more slender than in *Cardisoma* with spines on both margins of the palms and with granular to spinous fingers. The color is bluish gray with heavy maculations of reddish brown and purplish brown. It lives close to the sea in low-lying areas and among mangroves.

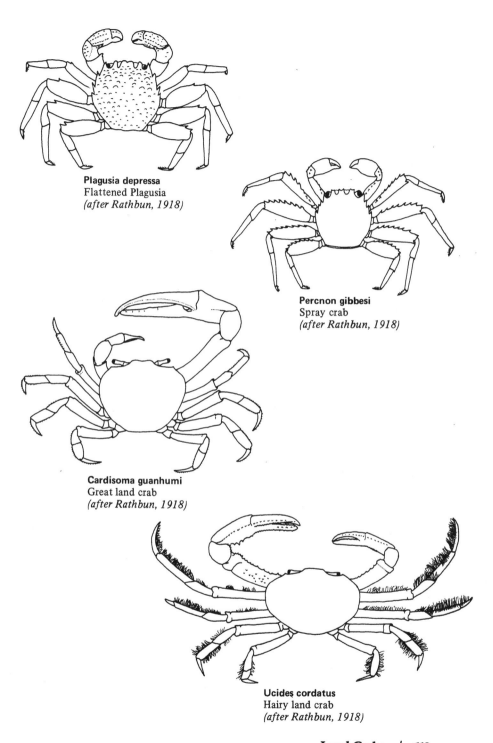

Plagusia depressa
Flattened Plagusia
(after Rathbun, 1918)

Percnon gibbesi
Spray crab
(after Rathbun, 1918)

Cardisoma guanhumi
Great land crab
(after Rathbun, 1918)

Ucides cordatus
Hairy land crab
(after Rathbun, 1918)

Land Crabs / 113

Black, blue or mountain crab   *Gecarcinus ruricola* (Linnaeus)

The carapace is strongly arched and has posteriorly converging sides. The last two joints of the walking legs are bordered on both sides by short, widely separated spines; there are six rows of spines on the dactyls. The chelipeds are equal in size. The claws are only slightly swollen, granulated, with somewhat slender, sharp fingers. In color the carapace is very dark, almost black, with a purplish tinge. There is a small yellowish spot near the posterolateral angle. The legs and claws tend to be reddish with yellow tips. This species lives in burrows in low-lying land near the sea. They are highly prized as food.

Black land crab   *Gecarcinus lateralis* (Freminville)

This is smaller than the preceding species and has a smoother carapace. There are four rows of spines on the dactyls of the walking legs, and the claws are markedly different in size in the males. The color of the carapace is deep reddish brown to plum color, often lighter posteriorly, with yellow spots. The legs are grayish brown while the claws are reddish with yellow hand and fingers. It lives in a much drier habitat than the preceding species.

FAMILY OCYPODIDAE

Sand crab, ghost crab   *Ocypode quadrata* Fabricius

This small crab is familiar to all who walk our sandy beaches, especially in the evening. It has a carapace width of about 2 in. (5 cm). The body is nearly square with a single sharp angle or spine at the anterolateral corners. The chelipeds are rough, scaly, or tuberculate. The legs are smooth, fringed on both margins by long yellow hair. The overall color is pale yellow or tan, imitating the color of the beach sand. It lives in small holes above the high tide mark and forages near the water's edge. It moves very quickly but is easily caught because of its habit of stopping in midflight and squatting on the sand.

Smith's fiddler crab   *Uca mordax* (Smith)

The species of this genus are very difficult to separate except by highly technical features. The large claw of the male of this species is nearly smooth with only a few coarse granules on the upper portion. On the inner surface of the palm an oblique ridge of tubercles veers upward to the carpal cavity. This ridge is several tubercles wide. This crab occurs on mud flats.

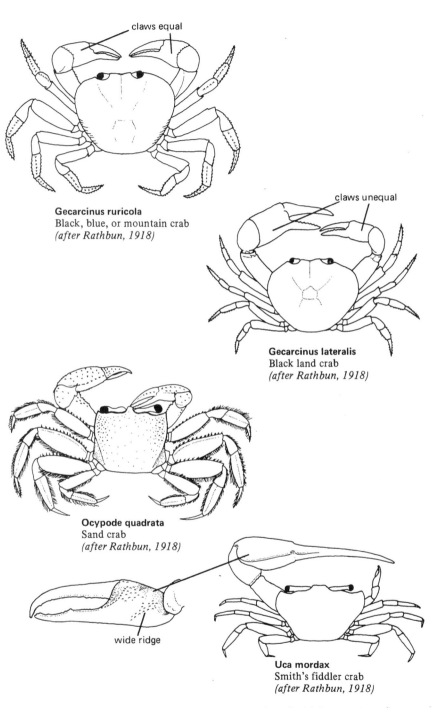

Gecarcinus ruricola
Black, blue, or mountain crab
(after Rathbun, 1918)

claws equal

claws unequal

Gecarcinus lateralis
Black land crab
(after Rathbun, 1918)

Ocypode quadrata
Sand crab
(after Rathbun, 1918)

wide ridge

Uca mordax
Smith's fiddler crab
(after Rathbun, 1918)

Land and Fiddler Crabs / 115

Rapacious fiddler crab   *Uca pugnax rapax* (Smith)

This crab is similar to the preceding species, but the large claw of the male is rough to finely granulose. The oblique ridge on the inner surface of the palm is narrow, and the whole inner surface of the palm is finely granulose.

Boxer fiddler crab   *Uca pugilator* (Bosc)

Although similar to the preceding two species, this crab is distinguished by the inner surface of the palm, which is granular with no oblique ridge. The large claw is rough and granulose. This is a common fiddler crab.

SUPERFAMILY OXYRHYNCHA
FAMILY MAJIDAE
The Spider Crabs

Arrow crab   *Stenorhynchus seticornis* (Herbst)

This delightful little crab is easily identified by its small triangular body and long, slender, spinelike rostrum armed on the sides by tiny spinelets. The legs and claws are long and slender, and the crab crawls slowly over the bottom, walking about delicately on algae-covered rocks and around reefs. The carapace is whitish or light tan with fine dark lines from the median line to the margin of the carapace. The fingers are blue, and the legs are spotted or banded with orange or red.

Riise's Podochela   *Podochela riisei* Stimpson

The knobby carapace is elongate-triangular with a long, shelflike rostrum from which the eyes project at right angles. The legs have numerous tufts of short hairs. The claws are rather massive. The body is brownish with several dark bands of brown on the carapace. The body is less than 1 in. (2.5 cm) long. This crab lives in grassy areas in shallow to moderate depths.

Spider crab   *Libinia dubia* Milne Edwards

The body is pyriform, terminating in a stout rostrum with two spines at the end. There are about six spines on each side of the carapace and a row of six small spines in a single row down the midline of the shell. The legs are moderately stout. The chelipeds are shorter than the walking legs, stout, with short fingers. The whole crab is dirty brown to yellowish. It lives on muddy shores and in shallow water.

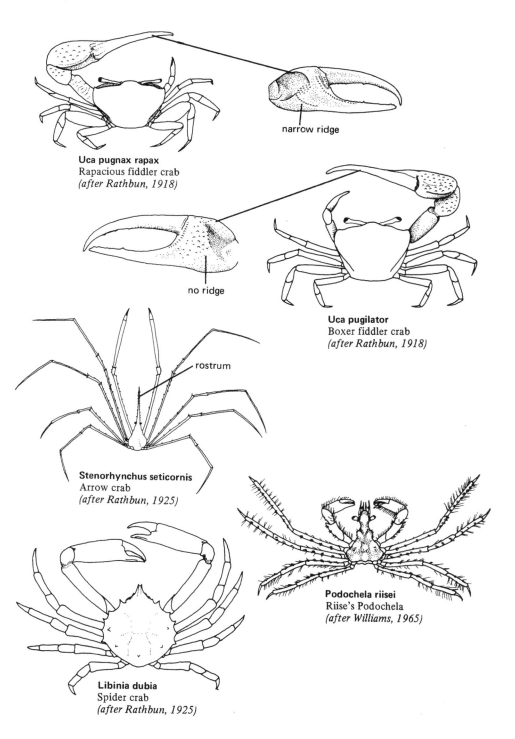

Uca pugnax rapax
Rapacious fiddler crab
(after Rathbun, 1918)

narrow ridge

no ridge

Uca pugilator
Boxer fiddler crab
(after Rathbun, 1918)

rostrum

Stenorhynchus seticornis
Arrow crab
(after Rathbun, 1925)

Podochela riisei
Riise's Podochela
(after Williams, 1965)

Libinia dubia
Spider crab
(after Rathbun, 1925)

Fiddler and Spider Crabs / 117

Gibbes' Pitho   *Pitho aculeata* (Gibbes)

This small crab, seldom exceeding 1 in. (2.5 cm) in length, has a broad, flat, frontal area between the widely spaced eyes, heavy claws, and five broad, obtuse, somewhat bluntly tipped spines on the lateral margin of the shell. The carapace is nearly smooth, variable in background color, but with maculations of greenish hues. The crab lives on sandy and muddy bottoms in shallow waters.

Martens' Pitho   *Pitho anisodon* (von Martens)

This is very similar to the preceding species except that the claws are slender and there are five acute, sharp spines on each side of the carapace. It has the same habitat, depth range, and geographical distribution as *P. aculeata.*

Spiny spider crab,   *Mithrax spinosissimus* (Lamarck)
cangrejo de la Santa Virgen

This is our largest spider crab, attaining a shell length of about 7 in. (18 cm) and a spread across the outstretched claws of about 2 ft. (61 cm). The nearly circular carapace, legs, and claws all bear spines and tubercles, those of the claws forming a single row on the upper edge of the hand. The color is reddish with lighter colored dactyls. It lives in and around rocks and rubble in shallow water.

Granulated spider crab   *Mithrax verrucosus* Milne Edwards

It is similar to the preceding species except that there are no spines on the hand of the claw and the upper surface of the carapace is closely covered with small, flat granules, which give it a paved appearance. The walking legs are hairy. The carapace length is about 2 in. (5 cm). It lives in shallow water near the shore where it hides in holes or under rocks.

Sculptured spider crab   *Mithrax sculptus* (Lamarck)

Similar to the other species of *Mithrax,* this crab has a smooth carapace bearing nodules on the posterior two-thirds. The wrist of the cheliped is smooth with no spines. The legs are very hairy. The color is greenish or bluish. The carapace of this small crab is under 1 in. (25 mm) long. It is found in shallow water on sand, shell, grass, and mud and both on and in coral reefs.

Decorator crab   *Stenocionops furcata* (Olivier)

The body is pyriform with two long rostral spines that curve inward toward each other. There are four lateral spines and one large, blunt median spine posteriorly. The legs are long, but the chelipeds are nearly

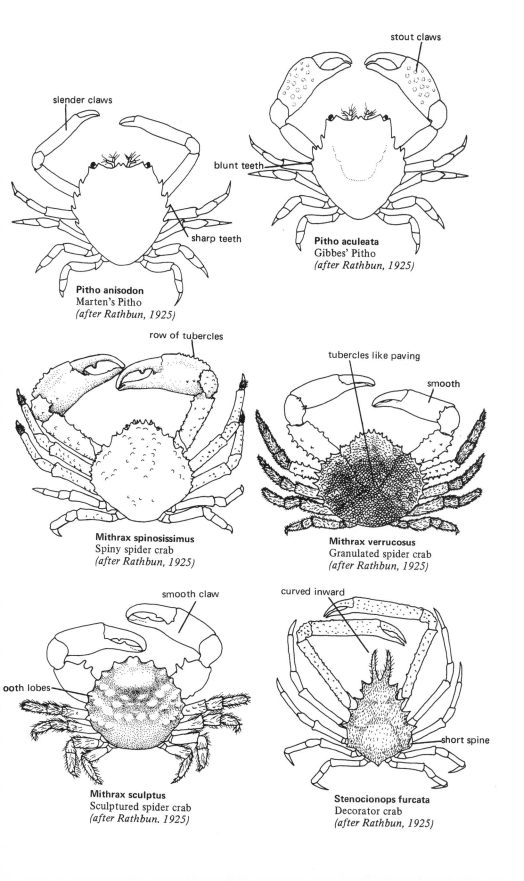

slender claws

Pitho anisodon
Marten's Pitho
(after Rathbun, 1925)

sharp teeth

stout claws

blunt teeth

Pitho aculeata
Gibbes' Pitho
(after Rathbun, 1925)

row of tubercles

Mithrax spinosissimus
Spiny spider crab
(after Rathbun, 1925)

tubercles like paving

smooth

Mithrax verrucosus
Granulated spider crab
(after Rathbun, 1925)

smooth claw

ooth lobes

Mithrax sculptus
Sculptured spider crab
(after Rathbun, 1925)

curved inward

short spine

Stenocionops furcata
Decorator crab
(after Rathbun, 1925)

twice as long with small fingers turned obliquely downward from the tubular palms. The carapace is covered with short, hooked hairs to which the crab attaches pieces of algae, sea grass blades, and other objects as camouflage. It has a shell length of about 6 in. (15 cm).

Grass crab, sponge crab   *Macrocoeloma trispinosum* (Latreille)
Decorator crab
The carapace is triangular with a broad rostrum ending in two long horns or spines. There is a stout spine on each lower corner of the shell. The surface of the carapace has four large, low knobs. The body and legs are densely covered with short brown hairs to which the crab attaches all sorts of objects; sponges, algae, and other sessile organisms. The carapace length may exceed 1-1/2 in. (38 mm).

Two-horned spider crab   *Microphrys bicornutus* (Latreille)
This is very similar to the preceding species, but the eye orbits are not expanded, the rostral horns diverge more, and the spine at the posterior angle is much smaller. The claws are conspicuously spotted. This species is very common on coral reefs and, like the preceding species, camouflages itself with a wealth of foreign objects.

FAMILY PARTHENOPIDAE

Serrate Parthenope, Elbow Crab   *Parthenope serrata* (Milne Edwards)
This unusual-looking crab has a flattened, small carapace covered with small nodules and bordered with spines. The walking legs are short, slender, and smooth. In contrast, the chelae are immense, long, flattened, and bordered on both margins by large acute spines. It may attain a width across the carapace of about 1-1/2 in. (38 mm).

ORDER STOMATOPODA
Mantis shrimp or Thumb-splitters

These are elongate crustaceans with narrow bodies and broad, powerful tail fans (telsons). They are unusual also in that they possess striking (raptorial) claws instead of the usual pincers. The raptorial claw consists of one primary, long, needle-sharp spine and a series of smaller spines on the inner edge. The telson is also armed with spines; if the animal is handled incautiously, it may inflict painful gashes, hence the West Indian name of thumb-splitter.

ROUTE ITEM

Title: Seashore life of Florida and the Caribbean / Gilbert L. Voss.

Author: Voss, Gilbert L.

Call Number: QL134.5.V67 2002

Enumeration:

Chronology:

Copy: 1

Item Barcode

A 8 6 8 0 1 5 6 0 0 3 7

Route To: .MAIN CIRC DESK
Carl Sandburg College Library
ILDS: CSC
Carl Sandburg College LRC
2400 Tom L Wilson Blvd

Galesburg
IL
61401
USA

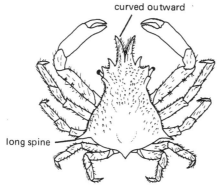

curved outward

long spine

Macrocoeloma trispinosum
Grass crab
(after Williams, 1965)

Microphrys bicornutus
Two-horned spider crab
(after Williams, 1965)

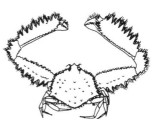

Parthenope serrata
Serrate Parthenope
(after Williams, 1965)

Stomatopods are active predators, either crawling about the bottom hunting for prey or lurking in burrows for passing unwary shrimp or fish. Some grow very large and are prized for their delicious meat; others are quite small. Some live in burrows in the sand, while other live in grass beds or on the reefs living under rocks or in holes.

Spider Crabs and Mantis Shrimp / 121

FAMILY SQUILLIDAE

Mantis shrimp   *Squilla empusa* Say

There are a number of species in the genus *Squilla*. *Squilla empusa* has five ridges on the carapace. The raptorial claw has six teeth. The telson has a blunt crest and six strong marginal spines. The body is usually pale greenish with the posterior margins of each segment bordered with dark green. The animal may attain a total length of over 6 in. (15 cm). It lives in sandy areas.

Ciliated false squilla   *Pseudosquilla ciliata* (Fabricius)

This is a small species attaining a total length of under 4 in. (10 cm). The raptorial claw is slender, the dactyl armed with three teeth. The telson is heavily armed with spines. The body is either yellow brown, bright green, or almost white. It commonly lives on grass flats or on the reef. A closely related species, *P. oculata,* has a pair of conspicuous large eyespots on the carapace.

Swollen-claw squilla   *Gonodactylus oerstedii* (Hansen)

The species of this genus may be immediately recognized by the swollen or inflated base of the dactyl of the raptorial claw. The dactyl is unarmed on its inner surface. The median keel or carina of the telson is large and swollen. The color is variable but usually is cream colored with light or dark green mottling.

Scaly-tailed squilla   *Lysiosquilla scabricauda* (Lamarck)

This is the largest of our mantis shrimp, attaining a total length of nearly 1 ft. (30 cm). The raptorial claw dactyl is armed with eight to eleven spines. The telson is covered with dorsal spinules and tubercles. The background color is cream with the body crossed at intervals by broad bands of dark pigment.

CLASS MEROSTOMATA

Horseshoe Crab

Horseshoe crab   *Limulus polyphemus* (Linnaeus)

The horseshoe crab or king crab is familiar to all sandbar waders and beach walkers. The smooth, glassy brown, almost circular, hinged body with its long spike tail may be as much as 20 in. (50 cm) long. It burrows along the surface of sandy bottoms in search of small animals for food.

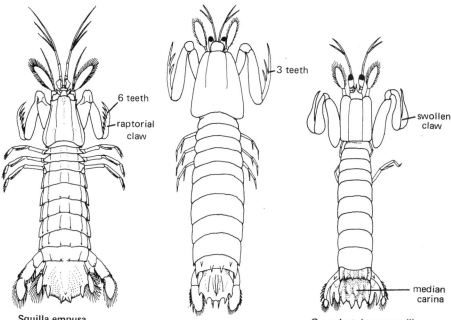

Squilla empusa
Mantis shrimp
(after Manning, 1969)

Pseudosquilla ciliata
Ciliated false squilla

Gonodactylus oerstedii
Swollen-claw squilla
(partly after Manning, 1969)

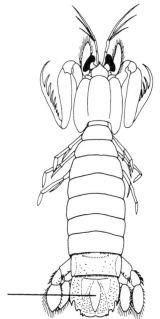

Lysiosquilla scabricauda
Scaly-tailed squilla
partly after Manning, 1969)

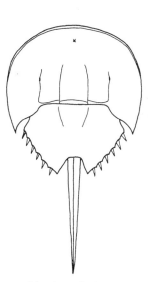

Limulus polyphemus
Horse-shoe crab

Mantis Shrimp, Horseshoe Crab / 123

Phylum Echinodermata
Sea Stars, Brittle Stars, Sea Urchins, and Sea Cucumbers

This phylum derives its name from the Greek words *echinos* "hedgehog" and *derma* "skin," in reference to the prickly surface of most of its members. While the larval form is bilaterally symmetrical, the members of this phylum generally show a radial symmetry of five radiating parts. The external skeleton or test is formed of calcareous plates closely united and often covered with spines. In the somewhat sausage-shaped sea cucumbers, these plates are degenerate and are buried in the leathery or fleshy body.

A characteristic feature of the phylum is the water vascular system, a hydraulic network terminating in a large series of tube feet which can be extended or contracted by varying the water pressure. These tube feet often bear a minute terminal sucker by means of which the animal can hold onto hard surfaces and even crawl about.

Echinoderms are important in marine food cycles. Starfishes may decimate oyster beds; sea cucumbers help to grind up calcareous bottom deposits but are eaten in the Orient; certain sea urchins produce eggs that are highly prized delicacies in the Caribbean. Many different species of echinoderms are dried and sold in curio stores.

The echinoderms are commonly divided into five classes: Asteroidea (starfishes), Ophiuroidea (brittle stars or serpent stars), Echinoidea (sea urchins, sand dollars), Holothuroidea (sea cucumbers), and Crinoidea (sea lilies). Numerous representatives of all these classes are found in south Florida and the West Indies, but Crinoidea are not discussed here.

CLASS ASTEROIDEA

Starfishes

The starfishes have somewhat flattened bodies. Most of the species are star-shaped with five or more arms. The tough skin has strong calcareous plates buried in it which may bear spines and tubercles. Scattered about among the spines and paxillae there may be pedecellariae, pincerlike organs, which keep the surface clean. The tube feet are found in a groove along the underside of each arm.

FAMILY ASTROPECTINIDAE

Two-spined starfish   *Astropecten duplicatus* Gray
    The body and rays are flat and covered with closely set paxillae that form a smooth mosaiclike paving over the surface. The rays are bordered by large, closely set plates of which the upper basal plates bear a single erect spine or nodule. The arms are moderately narrow and bluntly pointed. The color is gray or light brown. This starfish burrows in sandy bottom in shallow water.

Say's Astropecten   *Astropecten articulatus* (Say)
    This species is very similar to the preceding one but lacks the spines or nodules on the upper basal marginal plates. It varies in color from light brown to dark purple or reddish brown.

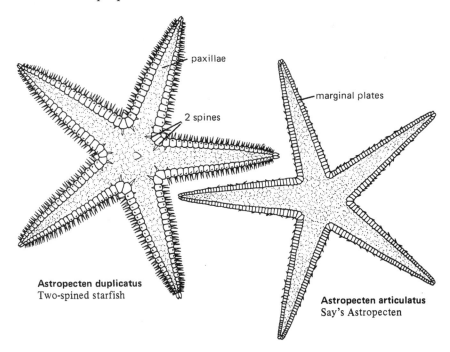

paxillae

marginal plates

2 spines

Astropecten duplicatus
Two-spined starfish

Astropecten articulatus
Say's Astropecten

FAMILY LUIDIIDAE

Nine-armed Luidia   *Luidia senegalensis* (Lamarck)
The most distinctive of all West Indian starfish, contrary to all others, it possesses nine arms instead of five. It is flattened, bluish gray or even greenish gray in color. It lives in sandy or sandy mud bottom in shallow water where it burrows after its prey. It attains a diameter across the rays of about 1 ft. (30 cm). It occurs from south Florida throughout the West Indies. It also lives on the West African coast from whence its name is derived.

Striped Luidia   *Luidia clathrata* (Say)
The striped Luidia is a very common species. It has relatively narrow arms. It is bluish gray above and whitish or grayish below, with a dark stripe of blue gray running the length of the dorsal surface of each arm. In some localities this color varies and occasionally the dark stripe is indistinct. It is found in sandy or sandy mud bottom throughout our range.

Banded Luidia   *Luidia alternata* (Say)
This handsome starfish is dark above, varying from greenish to purplish or blackish, variegated or banded with yellow or cream color. It is yellowish underneath. It occurs in sandy and sandy mud areas throughout our range.

FAMILY OREASTERIDAE

Cushion star   *Oreaster reticulatus* (Linnaeus)
The cushion star is the best known of all our starfish. It attains a width across the arms of about 18 in. (46 cm). It is deep-bodied with thick, short arms and a very strong, corneous covering. Young specimens may be olive green above, but as they grow older the color changes to brownish or orange red with the short, knobby spines the same color or yellowish. The ventral surface is yellowish to pale brown. It occurs on sandy bottom in relatively shallow water. It ranges from the Carolinas to Bermuda southward throughout our range. Because of its large size, color, and ease of collecting, it has become uncommon in some areas.

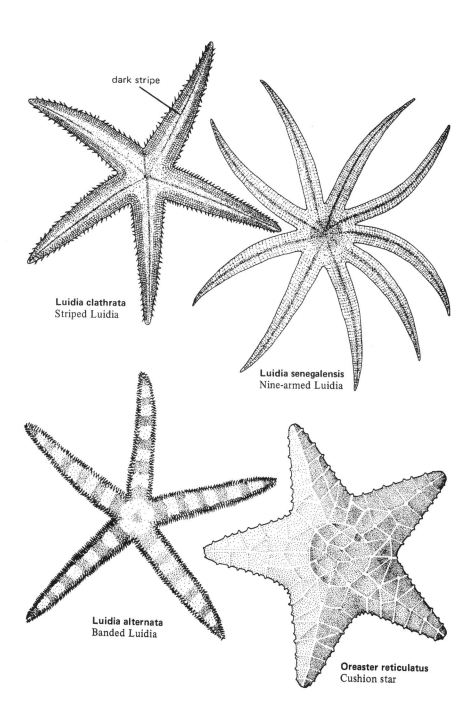

dark stripe

Luidia clathrata
Striped Luidia

Luidia senegalensis
Nine-armed Luidia

Luidia alternata
Banded Luidia

Oreaster reticulatus
Cushion star

Starfishes / 127

FAMILY OPHIDIASTERIDAE

Guilding's star   *Ophidiaster guildingii* Gray
This species has a rather smoothly knobbed surface covered with thick, raised plates that are arranged in regular rows on the disc and arms. In life it ranges in color from pale yellow through orange and even red. It attains a diameter of about 3 to 4 in. (7.5 to 10 cm) across the arms. It lives in rocky or reef areas from southern Florida throughout our range.

Common comet star   *Linckia guildingii* Gray
One of the most common starfish on the reef and reef tract, it has rather slender but swollen rays and irregularly placed, flattened plates. Its color varies in the young from dull reddish to brown or purple. Adults are more often reddish brown or a dull violet. This species is commonly found with one or more of the arms broken off. Often only one arm is still intact, but from the body end small arm buds arise forming a starlike pattern, thus giving it the name of comet star. The broken arms alone will produce new starfish. It often has six arms.

FAMILY ASTERINIDAE

Pentagon star   *Asterina folium* (Lütken)
This characteristic West Indian reef animal is pentagonal in shape, the rays not distinguished from the body. It is flattened, hardly more than 1 in. (2.5 cm) in diameter. It is often white but may range from yellow through reddish to even a striking blue. It lives under rock or in coral rubble and is sometimes secretive, burying in coral sand or in crevices.

FAMILY ECHINASTERIDAE

Thorny starfish   *Echinaster sentus* (Say)
One of our most common starfish, it lives in shallow water in grass beds, along the shore in rocky areas, or on the reef. Its surface is covered with small, widely spaced spinelets. The rays are rather short and blunt tipped. The color varies from deep red to reddish brown or dark purple.

Spiny starfish   *Echinaster echinophorus* (Lamarck)
This species is somewhat larger than the preceding one, the spinelets are smaller, more numerous, and sharper. The color is bright red. It is found in various localities in shallow water throughout the West Indies.

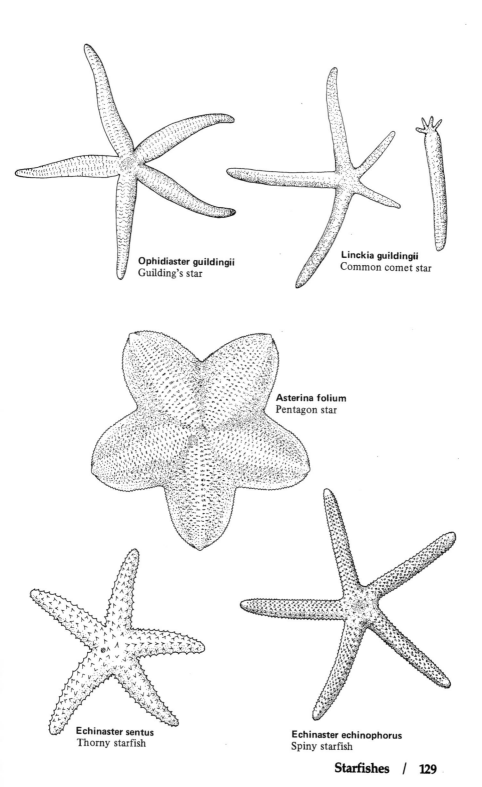

Ophidiaster guildingii
Guilding's star

Linckia guildingii
Common comet star

Asterina folium
Pentagon star

Echinaster sentus
Thorny starfish

Echinaster echinophorus
Spiny starfish

Starfishes / **129**

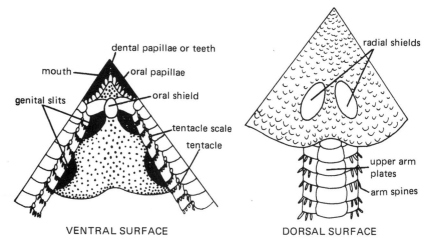

dental papillae or teeth

mouth

oral papillae

genital slits

oral shield

tentacle scale

tentacle

radial shields

upper arm plates

arm spines

VENTRAL SURFACE

DORSAL SURFACE

Diagram of sections of the disk of a brittle star

CLASS OPHIUROIDEA

Brittle Stars

The brittle stars or serpent stars have small, flattened bodies and very long, slender arms that are usually simple but in some are branched. They are called brittle stars because when handled the arms often break off. The skin may be smooth or covered with small to large scales, granules, or spines. Often the brittle stars bear plates, which give them an armored appearance.

FAMILY OPHIOMYXIDAE

Slimy brittle star   *Ophiomyxa flaccida* (Say)
    This is a large and active brittle star often found in shallow water behind and on coral reefs or in grass beds under rocks. The naked soft body is slimy to the touch. It may be as much as 5 in. (13 cm) across the arms. The color varies from dark green or brown, sometimes mottled with cream color, to orange brown or bright yellow. The disk and arms are naked.

FAMILY GORGONOCEPHALIDAE

Basket starfish   *Astrophyton muricatum* (Lamarck)
    This is the most easily recognized of all our brittle stars. Its arms are many branched, the hundreds of curling tips interlacing to suggest its common name. It lives in reef areas clinging to sea feathers and sea whips where it filters food from the water passing through its arm network. The color varies from dark brown to light yellowish brown.

Mud brittle star   *Ophionephthys limicola* Lütken

The disc is only about 1/2 in. (13 mm) in diameter, but the arms may be 10 in. (25 cm) long and very slender. The oral teeth are blocklike, and there is a single tentacle scale. The color in life is yellow green, often with a dark stripe down the arms. They may also be banded with red and black. It occurs throughout our range.

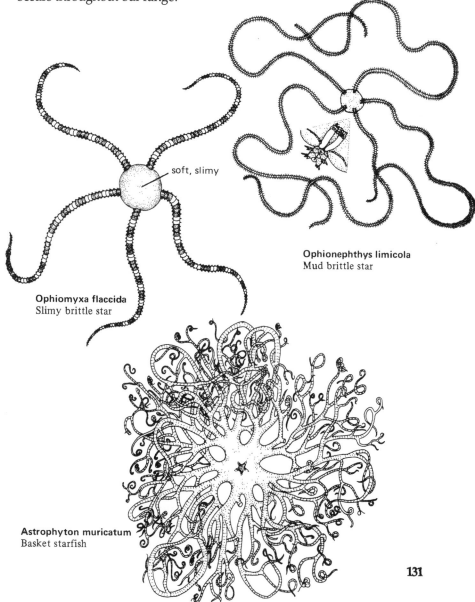

soft, slimy

Ophionephthys limicola
Mud brittle star

Ophiomyxa flaccida
Slimy brittle star

Astrophyton muricatum
Basket starfish

131

FAMILY OPHIACTIDAE

Sea grass brittle star   *Ophiactis quinqueradia* Ljungman
This small brittle star, only about 2 in. (5 cm) across the arms, is commonly found in clumps of algae or in sea grass. The disc and arms are dark reddish or purplish brown with variegations and bandings of white or gray. There is a pair of white plates on the disc at the base of each arm.

Savigny's brittle star   *Ophiactis savignyi* (Müller & Troschel)
This is one of our most common tropical brittle stars, living in sponges or coralline algae when young, in crannies and crevices or coral rock when adult. The young have six arms, adults five. The color is variegated green and white; the outer ends of the radial shields are white.

FAMILY OPHIOTRICHIDAE

Oersted's brittle star   *Ophiothrix oerstedii* Lütken
This is a rather common brittle star but varies greatly in color. It can always be identified, however, by the presence of fine lines of white crossing the upper surface of the arms. Otherwise, they may be dark gray, brown, purple, green, greenish blue, or cobalt blue. Specimens may have a disc width of over 1/2 in. (13 mm) and arms 3 in. (7.5 cm) in length.

Suenson's brittle star   *Ophiothrix suensonii* Lütken
This is one of the most beautiful of our brittle stars. It is somewhat similar to the preceding species, but the radial shields are large and bare and the arm spines are long, glassy, and thorny. The color is lavender, pink, or red; there is a conspicuous longitudinal arm stripe of deep purple or crimson, almost black. The width across the arms may be up to 10 in. (25 cm) but usually is much smaller. This species lives in and with gorgonians on the reef and reef flat.

FAMILY OPHIOCHITONIDAE

Reticulate brittle star   *Ophionereis reticulata* (Say)
A very common West Indian brittle star, it is easily recognized by the long, slender, whitish or pale yellow arms banded by brown or black and the small, bluish gray disc with, usually, a fine network of dark lines. It lives under rocks in sandy areas and occurs throughout our range.

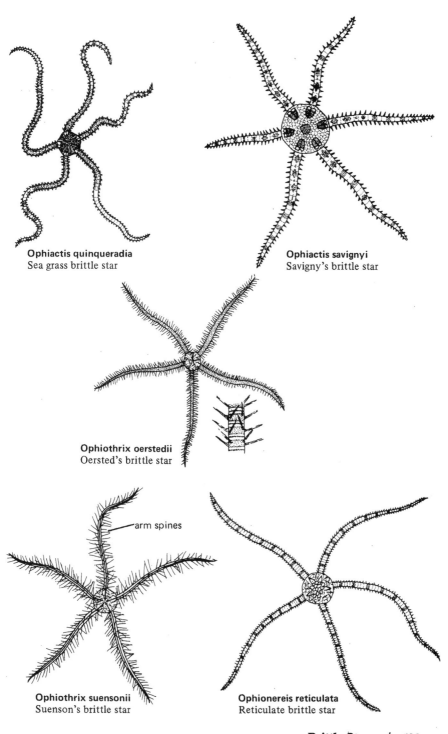

Ophiactis quinqueradia
Sea grass brittle star

Ophiactis savignyi
Savigny's brittle star

Ophiothrix oerstedii
Oersted's brittle star

arm spines

Ophiothrix suensonii
Suenson's brittle star

Ophionereis reticulata
Reticulate brittle star

Spiny Ophiocoma   *Ophiocoma echinata* (Lamarck)
This is a big, black brittle star with large outstanding arm spines. It is often variegated with white or cream color but never shows any reddish color. It commonly is 6 to 8 in. (15 to 20 cm) across the arms. It lives in shallow water under rocks and old coral heads on reefs or reef flats, or in grassy areas. It occurs throughout our range.

Red Ophiocoma   *Ophiocoma wendti* Müller & Troschel
It is similar to the preceding species, but it never shows any white or cream colored markings. It usually, however, shows some, to very strong, rust reddish casts to the disc, arms, and spines. It occupies the same habitat as *O. echinata* throughout our range.

Coralline brittle star   *Ophiocomella ophiactoides* (H.L. Clark)
This little brittle star is found in coralline algae in reef areas. It has six arms, usually with three arm spines in each segment, of which the uppermost is longer than an arm segment. It is yellow brown, sometimes with banded arms.

FAMILY OPHIODERMATIDAE

Snakeskin brittle star   *Ophioderma appressum* (Say)
This very common species is found under rocks or coral heads on reefs and in shallow water generally. Its color is very variable, grayish, brownish, or greenish, often with gray and white bandings. There are a number of closely related species inhabiting our range, such as *O. brevispinum*, which is very common in turtle grass and is often green with banded arms.

CLASS ECHINOIDEA

Sea Urchins, Sand Dollars, Heart Urchins

The echinoids are round or elliptical in outline with a hard calcium carbonate shell covered with numerous small to large spines. The test, as the shell is called, may be thin and very flat, as in the sand dollars or strongly arched as in the sea urchins. They live in a variety of habitats, rocks, sand, mud, grass, and coral reefs, from the low tide mark to the deep sea. They largely feed upon algae, sea grass, or incrusting plant life. These they scrape or cut from the bottom with their chisellike jaws

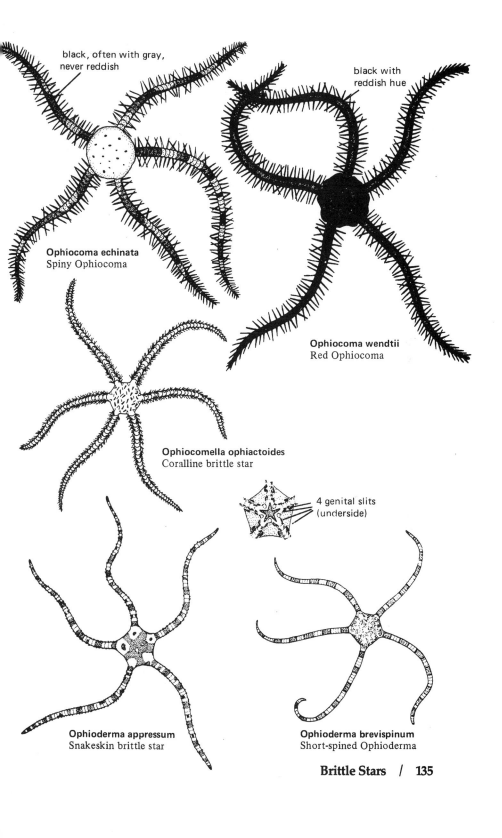

black, often with gray, never reddish

black with reddish hue

Ophiocoma echinata
Spiny Ophiocoma

Ophiocoma wendtii
Red Ophiocoma

Ophiocomella ophiactoides
Coralline brittle star

4 genital slits (underside)

Ophioderma appressum
Snakeskin brittle star

Ophioderma brevispinum
Short-spined Ophioderma

Brittle Stars / **135**

operated by the strange Aristotle's lantern structure within their mouth cavity. The bare tests of echinoids are often found on the beach and are eagerly collected by beachcombers.

Sea Urchins

The sea urchins have strongly arched tests and generally a circular outline. The dry, clean tests found on the beach show small to large round knobs or bosses, the basal attachment for the spines, and series of small holes or pores from which the tube feet are extended. If one of these tests is broken open, the basketlike Aristotle's lantern may be seen.

FAMILY CIDARIDAE

Slate-pencil urchin   *Eucidaris tribuloides* (Lamarck)
This species is easily recognized by its long, very stout, blunt, primary spines, which may be about as long as the diameter of the test. The other spines are very small. The color is usually light brown, striped or shaded with darker brown, and often marbled with white. There is often a greenish or reddish tinge. The large spines are often incrusted with algae, bryozoans, or sponges. This species occurs on reefs and in shallow water.

FAMILY DIADEMATIDAE

Long-spined urchin   *Diadema antillarum* (Philippi)
This is the most characteristic tropical, reef-dwelling sea urchin, well known to all swimmers and divers. It is best identified by the long, slender, exceedingly sharp and finely barbed spines that easily penetrate tennis shoes, swim fins, etc., and cause painful stings. The test of a large

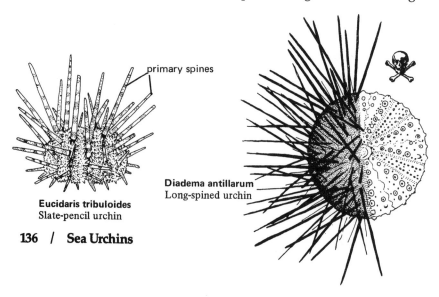

primary spines

Eucidaris tribuloides
Slate-pencil urchin

Diadema antillarum
Long-spined urchin

individual may be 4 in. (10 cm) in diameter with spines up to 16 in. (41 cm) long. The spines of adults are deep purple or black when alive; young urchins may have banded spines giving the animal a speckled appearance. They live primarily on coral reefs in clumps beneath sheltering objects. In some West Indian islands these urchins are so numerous that they form a black band surrounding the island, which is even visible from the air.

FAMILY ARBACIIDAE

Common Arbacia   *Arbacia punctulata* (Lamarck)
    The test is about 2 in. (5 cm) in diameter in adults, with spines about 1 in. (2.5 cm) long. Northern specimens are often colored deep brown with lighter colored spines while southern forms are varied, with a rather light brown base and spines which become darker towards the tip, to dull reddish purple or with test and spines reddish purple to nearly black. There are 4 plates around the periproct.

FAMILY ECHINIDAE

Variegated urchin   *Lytechinus variegatus* (Leske)
    This very common grass flat urchin has numerous plates around the periproct. It is commonly green and white; the color, however, is variable, and specimens are found that tend toward reddish purple and pinkish red, especially on the ends of the primary spines. The test may be 3 in. (7.5 cm) in diameter with rather short, stout spines. In most areas it camouflages itself by holding pieces of shell or mangrove or turtle grass leaves over itself by the upper tube feet. It feeds on turtle grass among other things.

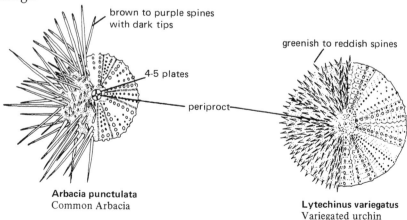

brown to purple spines
with dark tips

4-5 plates

periproct

greenish to reddish spines

Arbacia punctulata
Common Arbacia

Lytechinus variegatus
Variegated urchin

Sea egg *Tripneustes ventricosus* (Lamarck)

The largest of the tropical American urchins, it has a test that may be 6 in. (15 cm) in diameter. It is easily recognized by the numerous short, white spines that contrast strikingly with the brown to dark purple test. It occupies the same habitat as *Lytechinus*. The eggs of *Tripneustes* are edible and eaten locally wherever the species occurs. In Barbados its capture is regulated by law because of its importance as a food item.

FAMILY ECHINOMETRIDAE

Rock-boring urchin *Echinometra lucunter* (Linnaeus)

This species has an elliptical outline. It has short, thick, pointed spines. The color of test and spines is generally reddish brown though there is some variation; others may be almost black with a tinge of brown, purple, or green. This species usually lives in holes in rock along the shore at or near the low tide level.

Green rock-boring urchin *Echinometra viridis* (Agassiz)

This species closely resembles the preceding species but is distinguished from the latter most easily by the color. The test is elliptical, dark purplish brown, the smaller spines and the base of the primaries light brown with a reddish tinge. The primaries then become greenish, then bright olive green, terminating strikingly in deep violet or purple tips. It occurs throughout our range but apparently is not as common as *E. lucunter.*

Sea Biscuits and Sand Dollars

These are oval, elliptical, or round urchins with the test somewhat flattened and the periproct on the oral side.

FAMILY CLYPEASTERIDAE

Brown sea biscuit *Clypeaster rosaceus* (Linnaeus)

The test is oval, flattened underneath with a central concavity and arched on top with a characteristic five-parted, petallike sculpture centrally, clearly seen when the shell is cleaned of spines. The spines are short and closely set. The test may be as much as 5 in. (13 cm) long. The color is reddish, yellowish, or greenish brown or even dark brown. The dead, clean tests are usually snowy white. This is one of the commonest echinoderms and occurs in grass beds, sandy areas, and reef tracts.

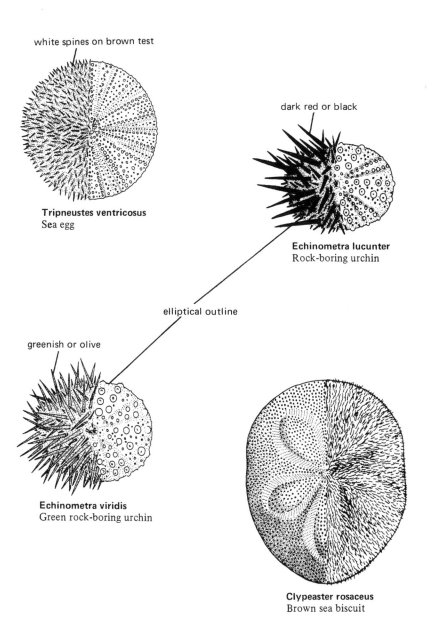

white spines on brown test

Tripneustes ventricosus
Sea egg

dark red or black

Echinometra lucunter
Rock-boring urchin

elliptical outline

greenish or olive

Echinometra viridis
Green rock-boring urchin

Clypeaster rosaceus
Brown sea biscuit

FAMILY SCUTELLIDAE

Sand dollar, arrowhead sand dollar   *Encope michelini* (Agassiz)
   The sand dollar is thin, hard, with the margins deeply to shallowly incised with notches. *Encope michelini* is higher in the posterior part of the test. It may reach a length of nearly 6 in. (15 cm). The color is deep violet brown both alive and dead. The test is thickly covered with very short spines that enable it to bury in sandy bottom. It is found in south Florida mainly from the Dry Tortugas up the Gulf coast and in Yucatán. A closely allied species, *E. emarginata,* with deeper marginal slits, occurs sporadically in the West Indies.

Key-hole urchin, key-hole sand dollar   *Mellita quinquiesperforata* (Leske)
   The common keyhole urchin is somewhat wider than long, thin, with a very flat test. It may attain a width of over 6 in. (15 cm). It is easily recognized by the five holes through the test. Specimens range in color from light brown to straw or sand color, sometimes gray. They are found in shallow, sandy areas.

Six-hole urchin, six-hole sand dollar   *Mellita sexiesperforata* (Leske)
   This species is very similar in appearance to the preceding one but attains a somewhat smaller size. It is immediately recognized by the presence of six holes through the test. It is silvery gray in the young, fawn to yellowish brown in adults.

FAMILY ECHINONEIDAE

Reef Echinoneus   *Echinoneus cyclostomus* (Leske)
   This is a very characteristic species of the reef tract, lying partially or completely buried in coral sand, usually under loose rocks. It is seldom more than 1 in. (25 mm) long. It is a very light cream to white color, sometimes brown, tinged with reddish, with conspicuous red tube feet.

FAMILY SCHIZASTERIDAE

Mud or burrowing heart urchin   *Moira atropus* (Lamarck)
   This species attains a length of about 2 in. (5 cm). The most characteristic feature is the very deep petal grooves in the upper surface; these are almost closed at the top to keep sand out of the respiratory area. It is colored dirty white or pale brown to gray. It burrows deeply into soft mud or sandy mud. It occurs from the Carolinas southward throughout our range.

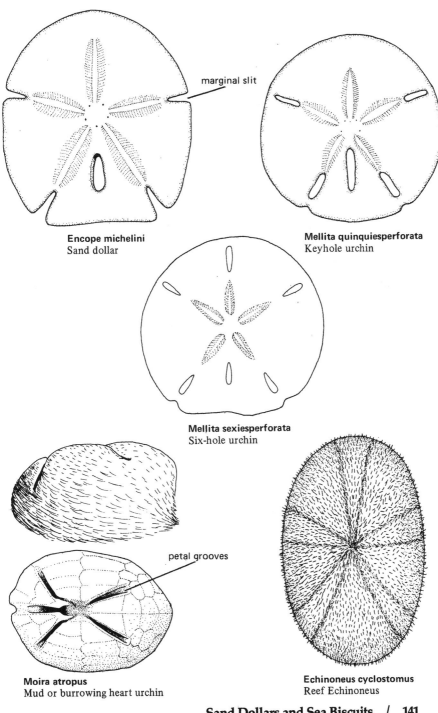

Encope michelini
Sand dollar

marginal slit

Mellita quinquiesperforata
Keyhole urchin

Mellita sexiesperforata
Six-hole urchin

Moira atropus
Mud or burrowing heart urchin

petal grooves

Echinoneus cyclostomus
Reef Echinoneus

Sand Dollars and Sea Biscuits / 141

West Indian sea biscuit *Meoma ventricosa* (Lamarck)
   This large sea biscuit, attaining a length of 5 to 7 in. (13 to 18 cm), is light to dark reddish brown. The test is thickly covered with short spines. It usually lives on the surface of sand or grass near coral reefs where it often covers itself with debris. It is often grayish in color from the coral sand on its upper surface. It is very common on the reef tract.

Long-spined sea biscuit *Plagiobrissus grandis* (Gmelin)
   This large sea biscuit attains a length of nearly 10 in. (25 cm). It is covered with medium-sized, sharp spines, of which those on the upper surface are much longer than the others, some attaining a length of 2 to 4 in. (5 to 10 cm), and are very sharp. Reputedly rare, this species is much more common than formerly thought. It lives in coral sand areas in the reef in depths of 20 to 50 ft. (6 to 15 m) or more, where it is fed upon by the larger species of helmet shells. It is a pale yellow to light tan with some reddish cast.

CLASS HOLOTHUROIDEA

The Sea Cucumbers

   Sea cucumbers are echinoderms in which the body has been drawn out along a longitudinal axis into a sausage-shaped form. The spines have been lost and the skeletal plates are reduced to small structures buried in the leathery body wall. They live on or partially buried in the bottom, feeding upon organic material in the mud and sand. If roughly handled or left in a collecting bucket in warm water, they may eviscerate or cast out their internal organs but they have the capability of regenerating a complete new set. Certain sea cucumbers are eaten in the Orient, where they are known as *trepang* or *bêche-de-mer.*

FAMILY HOLOTHURIDAE

Florida sea cucumber *Holothuria floridana* (Pourtalès)
   The species of this genus are so difficult to identify that skin preparations and detailed anatomical studies are necessary. This species reaches a length of under 10 in. (25 cm) and a diameter of 1 to 2 in. (2.5 to 5 cm). It is variable in color but is often a rather uniform brown or reddish, sometimes brick red. It lives in marine grass beds where it may be very common.

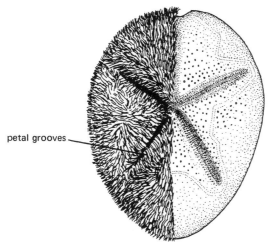

petal grooves

Meoma ventricosa
West Indian sea biscuit

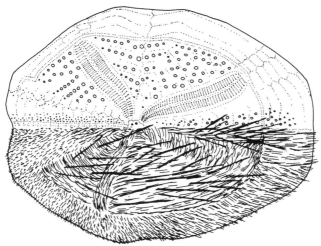

Plagiobrissus grandis
Long-spined sea biscuit

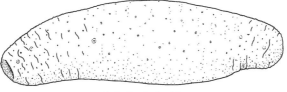

Holothuria floridana
Florida sea cucumber

Sea Biscuits and Sea Cucumbers / 143

Agassiz' sea cucumber   *Actinopyga agassizii* (Selenka)
This species is distinguished from all other West Indian sea cucumbers by the possession of five conspicuous calcareous teeth surrounding the anal opening. It attains a length of 1 ft. (30 cm), is robust, and is yellow brown, mottled with darker shades and dirty white below. It is found in grass beds and around reefs. It commonly is found with its commensal fish, *Carapus*, of which one or more may live in the cloacal cavity.

Four-sided sea cucumber   *Stichopus badionotus* (Selenka)
The animal is flat-bottomed in cross section, the bottom somewhat wider than the top with the angles rounded. The lower surface has three long bands of pedicels, but elsewhere they are irregularly arranged. The upper surfaces may be very rough to almost smooth. It grows to a length of about 10 to 14 in. (25 to 35 cm) and is about 2 in. (5 cm) wide. It varies in color from black to brown, deep red to purple, but mottled and spotted forms are common. It occurs in grass beds from the intertidal to a depth of about 6 ft. (1 m).

FAMILY SYNAPTIDAE

Sticky-skinned sea cucumber   *Euapta lappa* (Müller)
This is a long, wormlike sea cucumber, so extensible that measurements are difficult. It hides under old coral heads during the day. It has spicules projecting from the surface that cause the animal to adhere lightly to one's hand or arm when handled. It is light gray to light brown and covered with patches of white that give it a checkered or sometimes striped appearance. It makes an attractive aquarium animal.

Pourtalès' sea cucumber   *Chirodota rotifera* (Pourtalès)
This is a common species, rarely reaching a length of 4 in. (10 cm). In life it is flesh red with white, wheellike papillae. It occurs from Bermuda southward to Brazil.

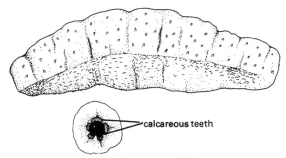

calcareous teeth

Actinopyga agassizii
Agassiz' sea cucumber

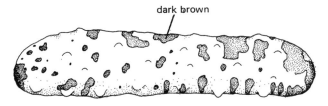

dark brown

Stichopus badionotus
Four-sided sea cucumber

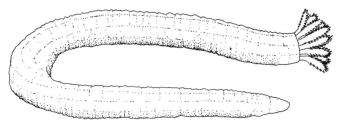

Euapta lappa
Sticky-skinned sea cucumber

Chirodota rotifera
Pourtalès' sea cucumber

Phylum Chordata
The Tunicates

The phylum Chordata includes the true vertebrates or those animals possessing a backbone (reptiles, amphibians,fishes, birds, and mammals) and a few odd animals, precursors of the vertebrates, that possess a primitive backbone (notochord) in the larval stage, as well as gill slits. The adults of these latter animals appear to have little resemblance to vertebrates and are not treated in guides to them. They are included here because of their general resemblance to invertebrates. There are four subphyla: Hemichordata, Tunicata, Cephalochorda, and Vertebrata. Only the Tunicata are included here.

Subphylum Tunicata
CLASS ASCIDIACEA
The Sea Squirts

The sea squirts would never be recognized as belonging to the Chordata if only seen in their adult attached stage. Essentially, the animal has a soft body enclosed in a sacklike outer covering, the tunic. This is unusual among animals for it is formed of cellulose, usually considered to be restricted to plants. This saclike structure is fastened to the bottom or a hard substrate while the free end has two openings. Water, along with plankton on which the animal feeds, is pumped in through one opening, passes through a straining apparatus termed the branchial basket, and is extruded through the outer opening.

Most ascidians are hermaphrodites. The eggs may be extruded into the

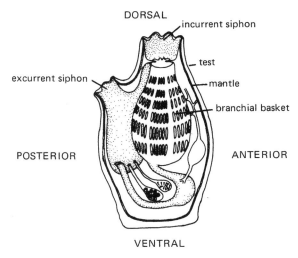

DORSAL

incurrent siphon

test

mantle

branchial basket

excurrent siphon

POSTERIOR

ANTERIOR

VENTRAL

Diagram of a tunicate
(after Buchsbaum, 1938)

open water or they may be retained within the parent. The larva closely resembles a frog tadpole and possesses a gelatinous, rodlike backbone, thus showing its relationship to the vertebrates.

Ascidians may form colonies or grow as separate individuals. They are found attached to wharf pilings, rocks, under old coral heads, on marine algae or sea grass blades, or covering mangrove roots. They may be drab in color, sooty blue black, or variegated with brilliant colors.

FAMILY DIDEMNIDAE

White sponge tunicate   *Didemnum candidum* Savigny

The colony is incrusting to massive, often forming grapefruit-size masses with the surface heavily and deeply convoluted. The tunic contains very small stellate spicules. The colony is hard, fibrous, and, despite the pores on the surface, is often mistaken for a sponge. The color is pure white to yellowish, rarely reddish, and sometimes discolored with mud. It lives in shallow water on the reefs or attached to hard bottom.

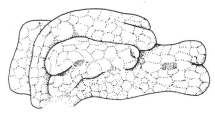

Didemnum candidum
White sponge tunicate
(after Van Name, 1945)

FAMILY POLYCITORIDAE

Painted tunicate   *Clavelina picta* (Verrill)
   The zooids or individuals are about 1/2 to 3/4 in. (13 to 19 mm) long and form clusters 1 ft. (30 cm) or more in diameter, which contain as many as 1,000 individuals. The tests or tunics are nearly transparent but are slightly opaque with a milky cast. Parts of the internal anatomy are colored purple or carmine. It is one of the most beautifully colored species when the zooids are fully expanded. It grows attached to alcyonarians, corals, and other hard objects in a few feet of water.

FAMILY PEROPHORIDAE

Mangrove tunicate   *Ecteinascidia turbinata* Herdman
   The colony consists of a thick group or cluster of elongate, slightly club-shaped zooids, each nearly 1 in. (25 mm) long and separate, united only at the base by a network of stolons. The tests are transparent and colorless, but the soft parts are often yellow, orange, or pinkish. They form dense clusters around the prop roots of mangroves and even on blades of turtle grass.

FAMILY ASCIDIIDAE

Black tunicate   *Ascidia nigra* (Savigny)
   This is the most easily recognizable of all our West Indian tunicates. It has a broad, leathery, thick, blue black test which may attain a length of 4 in. (10 cm) but usually does not exceed 2 in. (5 cm). It is solitary and usually found attached to rocks, sea walls, wharf pilings, and other hard substrates in shallow water.

FAMILY BOTRYLLIDAE

Flat tunicate   *Botryllus planus* (Van Name)
   The colonies are incrusting, irregular in outline, and usually so thin that the zooids are either half reclining or lying flat. The color is variable. The colony is generally dark, but the zooids may be purple, purplish brown, or blackish with the area surrounding the openings being white, pale green, or golden. Some colonies may be bright orange. The colonies are found on the underside of rocks, on corals, gorgonians, and turtle grass blades.

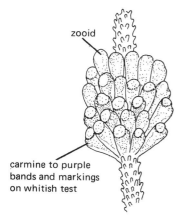

zooid

carmine to purple
bands and markings
on whitish test

Clavelina picta (on sea whip)
Painted tunicate

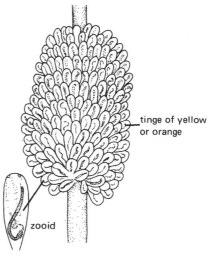

tinge of yellow
or orange

zooid

Ecteinascidia turbinata
(on mangrove root)
Mangrove tunicate

incurrent

excurrent

Ascidia nigra
Black tunicate

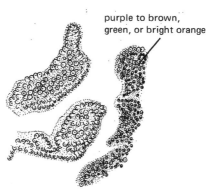

purple to brown,
green, or bright orange

Botryllus planus
Flat tunicate
(after Van Name, 1945)

Sea Squirts / **149**

FAMILY SYNOICIDAE

Stellate or starred Amaroucium   *Amaroucium stellatum* Verrill

This species forms large, platelike, irregular or spherical masses attached to rocks or shells. The colonies are hard, tough, and very smooth. The surface is covered with circular groups of pores, giving the surface a starred appearance. In life the colonies are pale bluish or sea green color. They are eaten by a wide variety of fish. The colonies often wash ashore after a storm, looking somewhat like slices of salt pork.

FAMILY STYELIDAE

Green incrusting tunicate   *Symplegma viride* Herdman

The colonies are similar to *Botryllus* in appearance, forming thin incrustations on sea grasses, algae, brozoans, and other objects when they may completely surround the branches and stems. The test is usually soft, transparent, and gelatinous. The zooids vary from purple to blackish or greenish, but the area around the openings may be white, pale green, yellow, orange, or salmon colored.

Incrusted tunicate   *Polycarpa obtecta* Traustedt

This solitary tunicate may be 2 in. (5 cm) long by about 1-3/4 in. (4.5 cm) wide. It has a tough, thick test often incrusted with sand and shell fragments. Those with clean tests are usually wrinkled and rough, often with warts or mosslike projections. The branchial openings are usually elevated and are conspicuously four-sided. The color in life is yellowish, brownish gray, or mud colored, darkening to purplish brown, brown, or red around the apertures. They live strongly attached to the underside of rocks or in shallow grass beds attached to stones, grass stems, and other hard objects. It is a common species from Bermuda to Brazil.

Divided tunicate   *Styela partita* (Stimpson)

This is a solitary tunicate that may attach singly or in clusters on wharf piles or on mangrove prop roots. The tests are tough and leathery, rough surfaced and often partly overgrown with algae and bryozoans. The color is grayish or yellowish posteriorly, turning brown, purplish, or red anteriorly, especially around the apertures. The apertures are frequently marked with alternating triangles of purple and white, the purple areas with the point upward, the white areas with the point downward. It closely resembles *S. plicata,* in which the apertures are square and heavily plicated and marked with radiating purple brown lines.

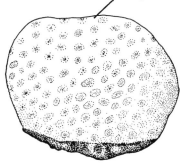

pale bluish or greenish

Amaroucium stellatum
Starred Amaroucium
(after Van Name, 1945)

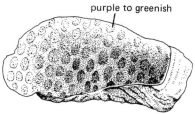

purple to greenish

Symplegma viride (on oyster shell)
Green incrusting tunicate

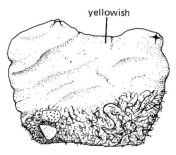

yellowish

Polycarpa obtecta
Incrusted tunicate

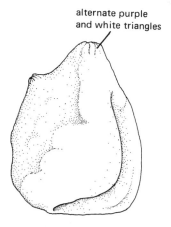

alternate purple
and white triangles

Styela partita
Divided tunicate

Sea Squirts / 151

FAMILY PYURIDAE

Banded tunicate   *Pyura vittata* (Stimpson)

This is a very variable solitary tunicate. It is roughly oval, usually less than 2 in. (5 cm) in length. The test is tough, opaque, and heavily wrinkled, and it is folded and covered with narrow, well-defined furrows. It may be incrusted with sand, shell fragments, or covered with other organisms. The color in a fresh specimen may be yellow to reddish or reddish brown, more intense around the apertures, which are often bright red. This tunicate is found in shallow water attached to stones and corals at or near the low tide mark.

Sandy-skinned tunicate   *Molgula occidentalis* Traustedt

This round to slightly oval, solitary tunicate is commonly found very loosely attached to mangrove roots, dead coral, and other hard objects but may live half-buried in mud and sand. The test is thin but tough and is usually of a sandpapery texture from the sand and fine shell incrusted in the skin. The color is usually that of the mud or sand in which it is found. When the surface is bare it is dingy yellow or gray, but it may be deep red around the apertures. It is often washed onto the beaches.

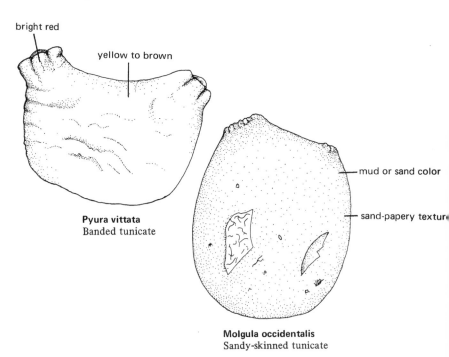

bright red

yellow to brown

Pyura vittata
Banded tunicate

mud or sand color

sand-papery texture

Molgula occidentalis
Sandy-skinned tunicate

Collecting and Preservation of Algae

Many of the remarks given in the section on collecting and preservation at the front of this book are pertinent to algae as well, and reference to that section should be made as needed. Algae require different collecting and preservation techniques, however, and these are discussed here.

Collecting algae is simple, and all the specimens described in the plant section can be collected, in appropriate localities, simply by wading. Attached algae can be pulled loose from the substrate or cut loose with a knife. The specimens should be floated in seawater in a bucket or placed individually in plastic bags partially filled with seawater.

As soon as possible after returning from the beach, you should either preserve or mount (press) your specimens. Preservation in liquid should be in 3 to 5% seawater formalin (see p. 14) buffered with borax. Labels (p. 16) can then be inserted and the bottles stored in the dark to prevent fading.

Specimens to be pressed should be cleaned of epiphytes, debris, and excessive branches. In a large, shallow tray half filled with seawater place a square of thin presswood or metal sheet and on it a sheet of heavy, good grade, high-rag-content paper or standard 11½ by 16½ inch herbarium paper. Press the paper to the bottom and on it float the algal specimen, arranging the plant as desired with forceps or dissecting needle. Tilt the board and paper slowly and gently allow the water to run off, leaving the alga in place. Final arrangement of branches and filaments may be done with a gentle stream of water from a pipette.

The mounting paper and algae should now be placed either on a large, thick sheet of blotting paper or several layers of newspapers. Next, lay a square of unbleached muslin over the specimen and another blotter or sheets of newsprint over this. Additional layers of blotters, specimens, and cloth can be stacked one above the other until all the algae have been prepared. To expedite drying, sheets of corrugated cardboard can be inserted at intervals. The collection should now be placed either in a plant press and drying box or a board and a heavy weight should be put on top of the stack. The blotters or newspapers should be changed daily until the specimens are dry. In warm, dry weather or in a dry room four to five days to a week are sufficient to complete pressing.

Soft, gelatinous, and finely branched algae will adhere permanently to the mounting paper. Cartilaginous, wiry, or calcified specimens may not adhere and will require careful gluing. A little care and experience will soon yield well-mounted, beautiful specimens for herbarium or wall decoration. Labels may be glued directly on the mounting paper, usually in the lower right-hand corner.

Coralline algae such as *Amphiroa, Jania,* and *Goniolithon* may be washed, dried, and stored in trays or other suitable containers. Cotton packing should be used to protect the more fragile specimens.

The Plant Kingdom
The Algae

Algae are simple plants that do not have true roots, stems, or leaves but may have parts that superficially look like them. What appear to be roots are holdfasts and do not derive nourishment from the substrate. The thallus or plant gains nutrients directly from the seawater and through photosynthesis in sunlight produces plant material. Reproduction is by means of microscopic spores rather than by seeds as in higher plants. Only the greens, browns, and reds are included here; the blue greens are beyond the scope of a field guide.

Phylum Chlorophyta
The Green Algae

The green algae are easily recognized by their green color, which is caused by the presence of the green pigment chlorophyll. They are very common in shallow tropical waters.

FAMILY ULVACEAE

Intestine alga   *Enteromorpha lingulata* J. Agardh

Pale to dark green, *lingulata* grows in tufts or tuft-like patches about 3 in. (75 mm) high, the individuals simple but usually branched. It grows attached to hard objects near the low tide mark from the Carolinas to Brazil. *E. flexuosa* (Wulfen) is similar but taller (10 in., 25 cm) and is single or in clusters, seldom branched.

Pale sea lettuce   *Monostroma oxyspermum* (Kützing)

The plants are thin-walled, consisting of a single cell layer, the cells visible in the thin sheet. This alga occurs as soft green tufts of flat to ruffled sheets attached to hard objects near the low tide mark and on mangrove prop roots. It may grow to a height of 1 to 4 in. (30-100 mm) but may be larger in protected areas.

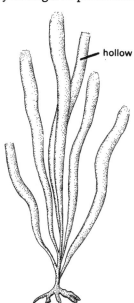

hollow

Enteromorpha lingulata
Intestine alga

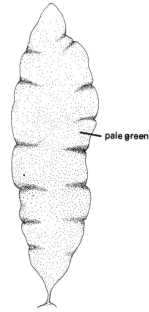

pale green

Monostroma oxyspermum
Pale sea lettuce

Sea lettuce   *Ulva lactuca* Linnaeus

Sea lettuce grows in flat to ruffled bright green sheets attached to hard objects or loose on the bottom. It can be distinguished from *Monostroma* by its thicker green sheets. It is often common in polluted or stressed areas. It may be separated from *U. fasciata* Delile by its simple or broadly lobed plant; *fasciata* is divided into narrow segments.

FAMILY CLADOPHORACEAE

Chaetomorpha Kützing

There are about 10 species of this genus in our range, all filamentous, soft, and often epiphytic. They form clumps, mats, or tufted branched plants. They should be identified using one of the standard manuals.

Cladophora fascicularis (Mertens)

This alga grows to a height of 1 to 1½ feet (30-50 cm). It is greenish, large and bushy with the branchlets curled downward. It grows on rocks or jetties from the Carolinas to Brazil.

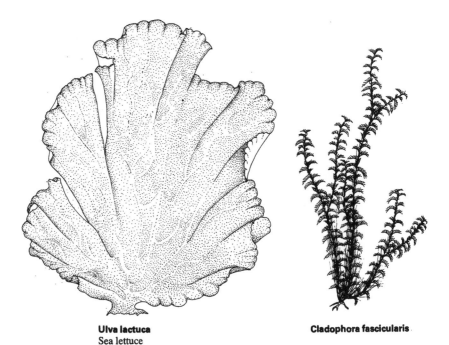

Ulva lactuca
Sea lettuce

Cladophora fascicularis

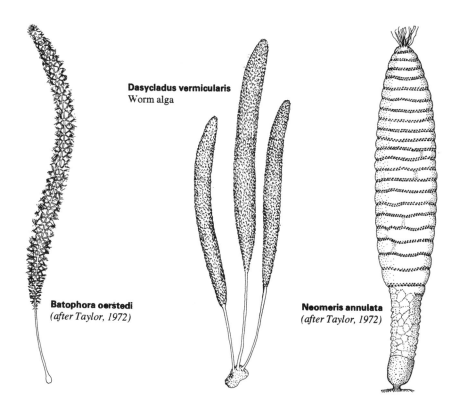

Dasycladus vermicularis
Worm alga

Batophora oerstedi
(after Taylor, 1972)

Neomeris annulata
(after Taylor, 1972)

FAMILY DASYCLADACEAE

Batophora   *Batophora oerstedi* J. Agardh
   The plants are bright green, soft, and grow singly or in clusters to a
height of 1 to 4 in. (30-100 mm). The plant consists of an axis with whorls
of branchlets evenly and widely spaced, all forming a soft cylinder from
¼ to ½ in. (6-12 mm) in diameter. The plants grow attached to hard
objects in sandy and muddy areas. When fruiting the stalk is covered
with small, bright spheres.

Worm alga   *Dasycladus vermicularis* (Scopoli)
   This is similar to *Batophora* but the plants are smaller, 1 to 2½ in.
(20-60 mm), and narrower. The whorls of the branchlets are crowded
together so that the plant has a velvety appearance. It grows on hard
objects and is often found around coral reefs and nearly buried in sand.

                                         Neomeris annulata Dickie
   This grows as solitary little plants that seldom exceed 1 in. (25 mm)
high and only about 1/16 in. (2 mm) in diameter. The main part of the
plant is calcified, whitish, and appears annulated or ringed. This interesting alga is often overlooked but may be common in shallow, clear, open
areas or tide pools.

Cymopolia   *Cymopolia barbata* (Linnaeus)
This unusual-appearing alga is formed of tubular calcareous joints.
The plants are whitish and sparingly branched, each branch ending in a
large tuft of green filaments. They grow in shallow water from Bermuda
to Puerto Rico and attain a height of 4 to 8 in. (10-20 cm).

Mermaid's wine glass   *Acetabularia crenulata* Lamouroux
This favorite plant of tropical aquarists is formed of small clusters of
slender, whitish to pale green stalks surmounted by one or more slightly
concave discs of fused rays with a crenulate edge. The clusters are attached to stones, shell fragments, or bits of wood. They grow to 3 in.
(75 mm) tall with discs to ¾ in. (20 mm) in diameter. Under normal
conditions the plants are a pale chalky green, but when sheltered from
the sun they are less calcified and greener. Four other species in our area
are all small with tiny discs.

FAMILY VALONIACEAE

Sea bottles   *Valonia ventricosa* J. Agardh
This alga forms large, thin-walled, round or elliptical sacs attached to
hard objects in shallow water and in turtle grass beds. The sacs are single
cells, among the largest known, and may be nearly 2 in. (50 mm) long.
They usually grow singly in contrast to *V. macrophysa* Kützing that forms
dark green masses of smaller cells, or *V. utricularis* C. Agardh that forms
bunches of lbranching, club shaped cells.

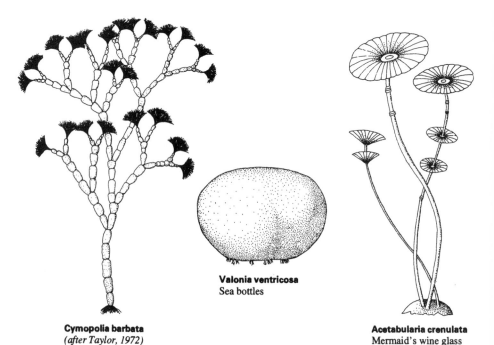

Valonia ventricosa
Sea bottles

Cymopolia barbata
(after Taylor, 1972)

Acetabularia crenulata
Mermaid's wine glass

Green bubble alga   *Dictyosphaeria cavernosa* (Forsskål)

The plant forms a large, green, hollow, nearly spherical mass that may be lobed or may collapse or rupture but continues to grow. The wall is crisp, crunchy, and shows large, angular cells. It may often form a large, saucerlike green plant. It grows in the intertidal zone and below.

Star alga   *Anadyomene stellata* (Wulfen)

The plants form erect, broad, flat, crisp blades of bright green attached to hard objects by a short, narrow stalk. When the blades are held up to the light, the branching, fanlike ribs can be seen. Under a hand lens the beautiful structure is plainly visible. The blades may be 1 to 4 in. (25-100 mm) tall and broad.

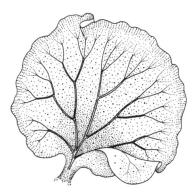

Anadyomene stellata
Star alga
(after Taylor, 1972)

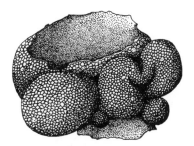

Dictyosphaeria cavernosa
Green bubble alga

FAMILY CAULERPACEAE

The Caulerpas, despite the great variableness of their branches, are easily recognizable by their long stolons or prone stalks with alternating branches and rootlike holdfasts. There are over 20 species of the genus in our range.

Caulerpa sertularioides (Gmelin)

This beautiful alga has long blades to 6 in. (150 mm) with closely set fine pinnules, giving it a feathery look. It is variable and has 4 named forms. It lives in open sandy areas.

Caulerpa lanuginosa J. Agardh

This odd-appearing *Caulerpa* has both stolons and branches densely covered with fine hairs, giving it a feltlike appearance. The branches may be 5 in. (130 mm) high. It lives in sandy areas.

Caulerpa cupressoides (West)

Eight different named forms have been described of this species. Most of them are characterized by long, flattened blades that appear closely serrate on both sides.

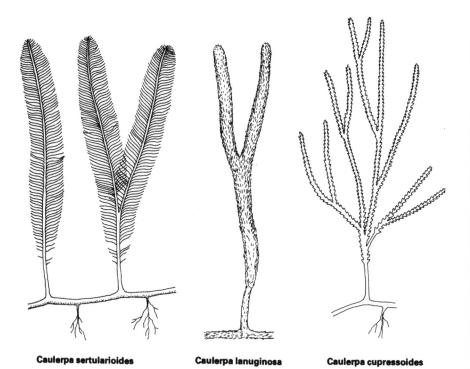

Caulerpa sertularioides　　**Caulerpa lanuginosa**　　**Caulerpa cupressoides**

Caulerpa racemosa (Forsskål)

This is the most variable of all the species of the genus, but the different forms all share in having the erect branches bear numerous clusters of small, berrylike green branchlets that range in shape from round to oval to elongate. They look like clusters of small green grapes.

Caulerpa peltata Lamouroux

These are small plants with short 2 in. (50 mm) branches with branchlets short and swollen, often ending in a little disc. They grow on rocks.

Caulerpa prolifera (Forsskål)

The erect branches are composed of a short stalk and broad, leaflike blade that may be single or branched. It often forms mats on the bottom.

Caulerpa mexicana (Sonder)

The erect branches are leaflike, with pinnate, closely set branchlets. The branches may be ½ in. (12 mm) wide and ½ to 8 in. (10-250 mm) tall. They grow on sandy and muddy bottoms.

Caulerpa ashmeadii Hay

This alga has broad pinnate blades with close-set pinnules. The blades may be 4 in. (100 mm) high.

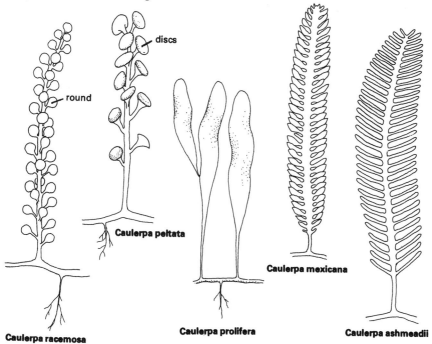

discs

round

Caulerpa peltata

Caulerpa mexicana

Caulerpa racemosa

Caulerpa prolifera

Caulerpa ashmeadii

FAMILY CODIACEAE

This family contains most of the calcareous algae, plants that deposit calcium carbonate to the extent that sometimes the major part of the plant appears whitish and stony. They are responsible for much of the calcareous sand of shallow tropical waters.

Avrainvillea nigricans Decaisne

These common plants of shallow, sheltered water are fanlike with thick, undifferentiated stalks. Although a green alga, it is usually dark brown or black. It grows to about 6 in. (150 mm) high with blades about 2 to 3 in. (60-80 mm) wide and long. It has several related species.

Mermaid's fan   *Udotea flabellum* (Ellis & Solander)

The plant is pale to medium green with a whitish cast caused by lime deposits. It is broadly fan-shaped with a short narrow stalk, but the blade may be branched, crenulate, or strongly folded. It displays several concentric growth lines. The plants grow to a height of over 8 in. (200 mm) and occur in sandy areas or in grass beds. *U. conglutinata* (Ellis & Solander) is more regularly fan-shaped, smaller, and found in depths down to 57 m.

Shaving brush alga   *Penicillus capitatus* Lamarck

This alga is one of the most common in shallow, warm bays and lagoons. It has a short stalk 1 to 4 in. (30-100 mm) tall, surmounted by a head or capitulum 1 to 1¼ in. (20-30 mm) long. The stalk is heavily calcified and grayish whereas the head is pale to medium whitish green. It may form large colonies or be mixed with seagrasses. *P. dumetosus* (Lamouroux) is similar, but the stalk is shorter and the head larger and looser. It is not so heavily calcified.

Rhipocephalus phoenix (Ellis & Solander)

This resembles *Penicillus* but the filaments of the head are not separate and loose but are fused into radially arranged platelets. It is somewhat calcified, dull green, and attains a height of about 3 to 5 in. (70-120 mm).

The Halimedas

The halimedas are important shallow water calcareous algae that often form dense mats or beds offering refuge for a host of invertebrate animals. The dead joints of the calcareous branches form important and characteristic sediments among and behind coral reefs and in shallow water. There are 10 species and numerous forms in the Caribbean, and Taylor, 1972, should be consulted for other species than those described here.

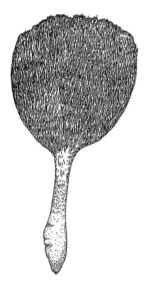

Avrainvillea nigricans

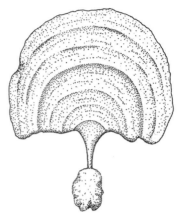

Udotea flabellum
Mermaid's fan

Penicillus capitatus
Shaving brush

Rhipocephalus phoenix

Halimeda opuntia (Linnaeus)
The plants are heavily calcified, whitish green, and grow to a height of 4 to 10 in. (100-250 mm). The calcified joints are variable in shape but often are 2- to 3-lobed. The branches are numerous and are in different planes. They grow on rocks, broken shell, and in sand.

Halimeda tuna (Ellis & Solander)
This species is less calcified and the plants are greener, often dark green. The branches are in one plane, and the joints are large, flat, and round to kidney-shaped. They grow to a height of 4 to occasionally 10 in. (100-250 mm).

Halimeda incrassata (Ellis)
The plants have a well-developed, thick, heavily calcified stalk above which the branches are more or less in one plane. The plants are erect, and the joints are flat, usually 3-lobed, and ribbed. They are dull green in the upper portions, whitish near the base. They grow to a height of about 8 to 9 in. (200-240 mm).

Halimeda monile (Ellis & Solander)
The plants are bushy, heavily calcified, and dark green. The lower branches are sparse and the segments flattened and irregular. The upper branches are numerous, and near the ends the segments are cylindrical. They grow to a height of 4 to 10 in. (100-250 mm).

Codium isthmocladum Vickers
These bushy, light green plants are dichotomously (always in two) branched many times, the branches round and tapering. They are smooth, often slippery to the touch. They grow erect to a height of 8 in. (200 mm) on rocks and dead coral.

Codium decorticatum (Woodward)
This large alga may be 3 feet (1 m) tall. It is light green, sparingly branched basally but may be profusely branched near the ends. The dichotomous branching occurs at broadly flattened areas although the branches between may be slender. *C. taylori* Silva is profusely branched with short stiff branches. It is dark green. Both grow throughout our range.

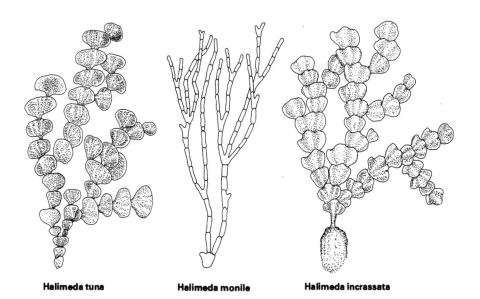

Halimeda tuna   **Halimeda monile**   **Halimeda incrassata**

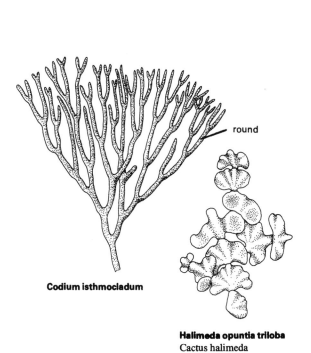

round

Codium isthmocladum

Halimeda opuntia triloba
Cactus halimeda

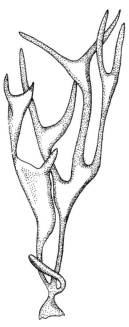

Codium decorticatum
(after Taylor, 1972)

Green Algae / 165

Phylum Phaeophyta
The Brown Algae

In this group the green chlorophyll is mostly masked by the brown pigment fucoxanthin. With the exception of the sargassums, the large brown algae, such as the kelps, are not found in tropical waters.

FAMILY ECTOCARPACEAE

Ectocarpus spp.

Several species of this genus are in our area, most of which are epiphytic, growing on other algae or marine grasses. They usually appear as soft, brown tufts. They are difficult to identify except by a specialist using a microscope.

FAMILY DICTYOTACEAE

Dictyota dichotoma (Hudson)

This bushy, brown alga grows only to a height of about 1½ to 4 in. (35-100 mm) with flat, straplike branches always branching dichotomously (in twos). The blades are 2 to 5 mm broad and from 10 to 25 mm between branching.

Dictyota dentata Lamouroux

The plants are bushy, erect to 4 to 8 in. (100-200 mm), with a central axis and alternately spaced branches. The branches are more or less in one plane and the branches and branchlets are straplike. Most of the tips of the branchlets end in spurlike projections, hence the name.

Dictyota bartayresii Lamouroux

These small, bushy plants form masses 2 to 8 in. (50-200 mm) across and branch in twos. They are crisp, light brown, and easily damaged. They are very common attached to hard objects.

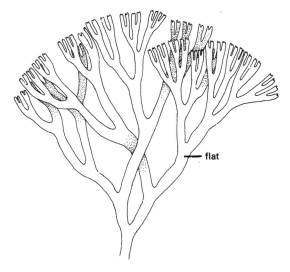

Dictyota dichotoma

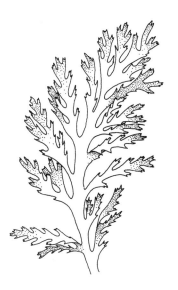

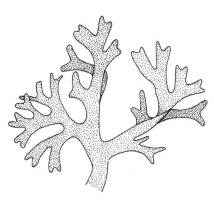

Dictyota bartayresii

Dictyota dentata
(after Taylor, 1972)

Pocockiella variegata (Lamouroux)

This is a small, light brown alga consisting of blades that are round or kidney-shaped attached directly to hard objects. The blades are thin and contain one or more crescentric lines. It grows to a height of 1¼ to 3¼ in. (30-80 mm).

Stypopodium zonale (Lamouroux)

This alga is a strongly iridescent brown in life. It is formed of broad, flat branches becoming many branched and fanlike terminally. The blades are zoned or crossed by dark lines at frequent intervals. It occurs from the intertidal zone downward. It may be 12 in. (30 cm) high. An older name is *Zonaria zonalis*.

Padina sanctaecrucis Børgesen

This alga forms curled, fanlike branches from a single stalk, the plant about 6 in. (15 cm) tall. The upper surfaces of the fans are calcified and whitened, but the rest of the plant is brownish. All the branches are crossed by closely set growth lines. *P. vickersiae* Hoyt is similar, but the concentric lines are farther apart and calcification is very light.

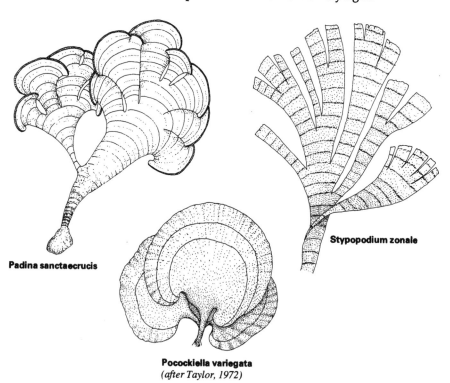

Padina sanctaecrucis

Stypopodium zonale

Pocockiella variegata
(after Taylor, 1972)

FAMILY SARGASSACEAE
Sargassum or Gulfweed

Gulfweed is familiar to every beach walker, and boatmen encounter great floating masses of it at sea. There are 15 species from our waters. Only the most common are described here.

Gulfweed   *Sargassum filipendula* C. Agardh

These are golden brown plants growing attached to hard substrate and attaining heights of up to 6 feet (2 m). The leaves are serrate, 3/16 to ⅜ in. (5-8 mm) wide and 1 to 3¼ in. (20-80 mm) long. The air floats or bladders are round, 3 to 5 mm in diameter, with stalks about 5 mm long.

Gulfweed   *Sargassum fluitans* Børgesen

This brown alga is pelagic, and attached stages are unknown. The leaves are short stalked, ¾ to 2¼ in. (20-60 mm) long and ⅛ to ⅜ in. (3-8 mm) wide and serrate. The air bladders or floats are round to oval, about 4 to 5 mm in diameter on short stalks only 2 to 3 mm long. The ends of the floats are smooth.

Sargassum filipendula
Gulfweed
(after Taylor, 1972)

Sargassum fluitans
Gulfweed
(after Taylor, 1972)

Gulfweed   *Sargassum natans* (Linnaeus)
The leaves are long and slender, 1/16 in. (2-3.5 mm) wide by 1 to 2¾ in. (25-70 mm) long with sharp, slender teeth as long as the width of the blade. The air bladders are 3 to 5 mm in diameter, usually with a long spine or spur growing out of the outer surface. They are pelagic plants and are unknown attached.

Turbinaria turbinata (Linnaeus)
This easily identified alga has an axial stem up to 12 in. (30 cm) or more, around which pyramidal-shaped leaves are clustered at intervals. The ends of these leaves are squarish with sharp points at the angles and with a mound in the center containing an air float.

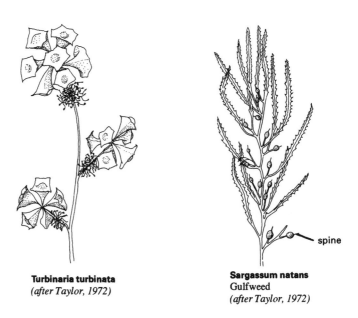

spine

Turbinaria turbinata
(after Taylor, 1972)

Sargassum natans
Gulfweed
(after Taylor, 1972)

Phylum Rhodophyta
The Red Algae

It is sometimes difficult to determine if a plant is a red alga as the reddish color of the phycoerythrin may be obscured by brown or green pigments. All reds when alive, however, will show at least a pinkish color at the growing tips. Pink or red colors do not occur in the other two groups.

FAMILY HELMINTHOCLADIACEAE

Liagora farinosa Lamouroux

The plants are bushy and dichotomously branched. They are calcified throughout but only lightly in the upper part. They are reddish, pale toward the holdfast. They grow to a height of 5 in. (120 mm) or higher attached on hard objects in sheltered waters.

FAMILY CHAETANGIACEAE

Galaxaura marginata (Ellis & Solander)

Young plants are reddish, but older ones become dull colored or grayish from calcification. They grow to 2 to 6 in. (50-140 mm) and are branched dichotomously. The branches appear to be banded and may end in a tuft of soft, pinkish hairs.

FAMILY GELIDIACEAE

Gelidiella acerosa (Forsskål)

Colored greenish yellow to dull purple, these plants are tall, 2 to 6 in. (50-140 mm), sparingly branched, and wiry. The long branches sprawl on the bottom with short branchlets on the ends growing upward.

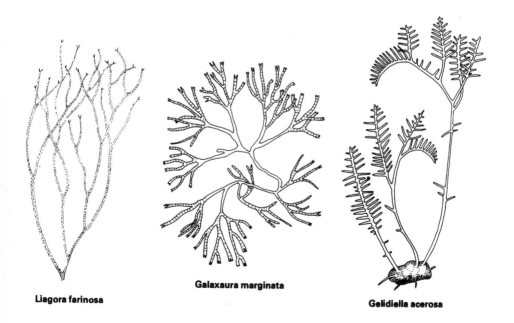

Galaxaura marginata

Liagora farinosa

Gelidiella acerosa

FAMILY CORALLINACEAE
The Corallines

The coralline algae are reds that are so heavily calcified that some have lost all superficial resemblance to plants and are often thought to be some type of coral. They are difficult to identify except by sectioning and microscopic examination.

Coralline   *Lithothamnion* spp.

A dozen species of this genus occur within our range. They vary from encrusting forms coating over dead coral to forms that both encrust and grow upward as stony, branching plants. They vary in color from white through pink to vinous purple and are commonly seen on coral reefs, where they play an important role in cementing the soft coral fragments.

Coralline   *Goniolithon* spp.

Similar to the above genus, *Goniolithon* forms mainly hard encrustations on rocks and dead coral. They are generally light pink to purple. They may also form irregular knobbed lumps on dead coral or fragile masses of closely entangled thin branches, such as *Goniolithon strictum* Foslie, often collected as some type of coral. *G. spectabilis* Foslie forms more solid masses from which only the tips of the branches project.

Fragile coralline   *Amphiroa fragilissima* (Linnaeus)

This delicate coralline, white or slightly pinkish, often forms extensive mats 1 to 2 in. (25-50 mm) tall in protected areas behind reefs or in quiet bay waters. The branchlets are slender and always branch dichotomously in the joint itself. The beds are found near the low water mark and are crunchy under foot.

Red coralline   *Jania rubens* (Linnaeus)

The plants are rose red, growing to a height of 1 to 2 in. (25-50 mm). The branches are delicate, slender, and have pointed tips. The branching is narrow with only a slight angle.

FAMILY GRACILARIACEAE

Gracilaria verrucosa (Hudson)

This alga is bushy, growing to 12 in. (300 mm). While it starts life attached to hard objects, it often becomes free and floats or lies on the bottom. It is greenish translucent, grayish, or dull purplish red. Branching is irregular. The tips of the branchlets are slender and pointed.

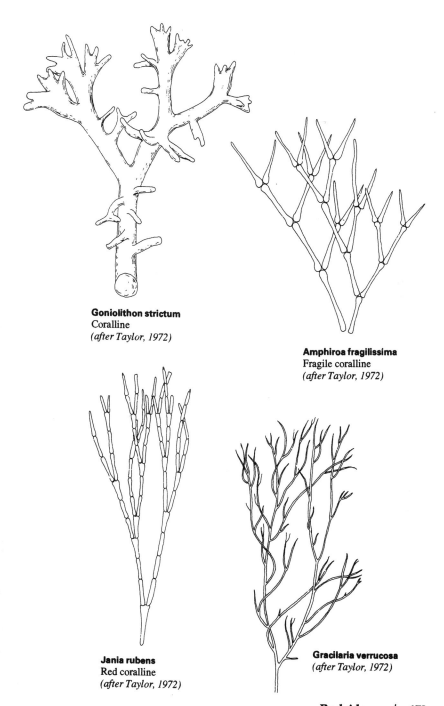

Goniolithon strictum
Coralline
(after Taylor, 1972)

Amphiroa fragilissima
Fragile coralline
(after Taylor, 1972)

Jania rubens
Red coralline
(after Taylor, 1972)

Gracilaria verrucosa
(after Taylor, 1972)

Red Algae / 173

FAMILY SOLIERIACEAE

Agardhiella tenera (J. Agardh)

These are bushy and grow to about 1 foot (300 mm) tall. They are pinkish translucent to a deep rose red and have a fleshy feel. Branching is radial with the branches smaller at the ends and swollen in the middle.

Eucheuma isiforme (C. Agardh)

These are large algae growing to 1½ to 2 feet (45-60 cm) tall. They are strong, have a cartilaginous appearance and feel and are a pale yellow to yellowish brown to reddish. Branching is irregular. The branchlets are small, knobby, irregular, often spiny and whorled.

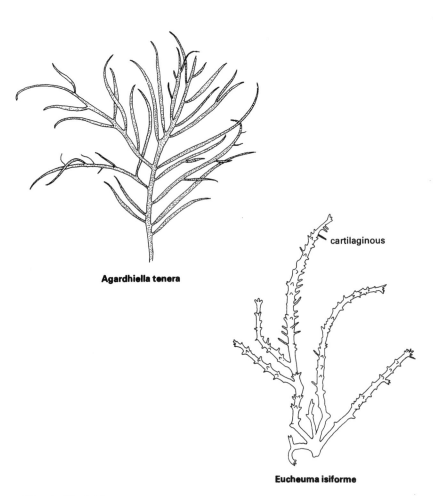

Agardhiella tenera

cartilaginous

Eucheuma isiforme

FAMILY HYPNEACEAE

Hypnea musciformis (Wulfen)

The plants are bushy with slender branches that have numerous threadlike branchlets throughout their length. Color is pale pink to purplish red. A characteristic feature is the swollen, strongly curved hooks on the tips of most of the branches. None of the other three species possess these swollen hooks. They are supposed to be clasping organs.

FAMILY CERAMIACEAE

Ceramium fastigiatum (Roth)

There are about 18 species of this genus in our range. Most are small to minute and require preparation and microscopic examination for identification. This species is a bright rose red tuft of fine filaments 1½ to 3 in. (40-80 mm) long, which grows attached to coarse algae, sea grasses, and mangrove prop roots. It is soft and cottony.

FAMILY DASYACEAE

Dasya pedicellata (C. Agardh)

The plants are tall, 8 to 28 in. (200-700 mm), growing from a disclike holdfast. They are pale to dark reddish purple and are sparingly alternately branched. The branches are long and drooping, graceful, covered with short, hairlike filaments.

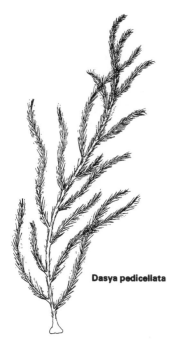

Dasya pedicellata

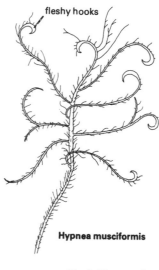

fleshy hooks

Hypnea musciformis

FAMILY RHODOMELIACEAE

Digenia simplex (Wulfen)

The plants are 1 to 10 in. (30-250 mm) tall, sparsely branched, wiry to cartilaginous. The branches are clothed with slender, stiff branchlets. This alga is commonly covered by epiphytic algae so that it often is completely hidden.

Chondria tenuissima (Goodenough & Woodward)

This peculiar alga may be easily recognized by its spindle-shaped branchlets attached to the few sparse branches. The branches are coarse and firm, but the branchlets are soft. The plants grow to a height of 4 to 8 in. (100-200 mm) on rocks or shell fragments. They are straw color to dull purple.

Acanthophora spicifera (Vahl)

The plants are tall, to 10 in. (250 mm), sparsely branched and somewhat bushy. The branches are covered with small, spinous branchlets, little protruding from the branches. They have a cartilaginous consistency and are prickly from the spines. The color is greenish yellow to dark red.

Laurencia papillosa (Forsskål)

The plants are densely clustered, olive green to greenish purple and somewhat cartilaginous. They grow to about 2 to 6 in. (50-160 mm) tall. The lower parts of the plants are smooth, but toward the ends the branches are sparsely to densely crowded with short, truncate to tuberculate branchlets.

Laurencia poitei (Lamouroux)

The plants are about 4 in. (100 mm) tall and pale buff to pinkish or brownish. The main axis is alternately branched, the branches cartilaginous. The outer branches bear small, fat branchlets that are truncated or squared at the ends. This species may be very common in protected waters and are frequently found as "rollers" on the bottom, forming rolls a meter in diameter that are moved about by wave and tidal currents.

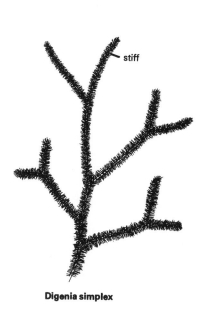

Digenia simplex

stiff

Chondria tenuissima
(after Dawes, 1974)

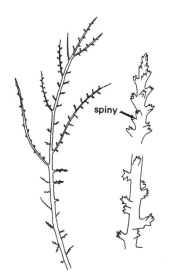

spiny

Acanthophora spicifera

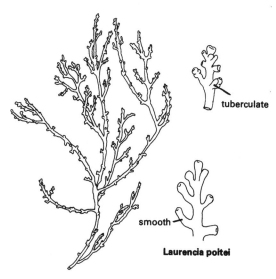

tuberculate

smooth

Laurencia poitei

Laurencia papillosa
(after Hillson, 1977)

Red Algae / 177

Phylum Tracheophyta
Marine Phanerogams

Sea Grasses

The sea grasses are phanerogams or true flowering plants that live in shallow seas. They form vast meadows now known to be nursery grounds of many important invertebrates and fishes. Unlike the algae, they have true roots, stems, leaves, and flowers.

FAMILY RUPPIACEAE

Widgeon or ditch grass *Ruppia maritima* Linnaeus
The plants have long, dark green stems rising from long rhizomes or runners with few weak roots. The leaves are long, 2 to 4 in. (40-100 mm), with a single vein and are flat. They taper to long, slender tips. The flowers are inconspicuous, and the fruit are borne on the ends of long, slender stalks. It grows in both brackish and saline waters.

FAMILY CYMODOCEAE

Manatee grass *Cymodocea filiforme* Kützing
The rhizomes lie flat on the bottom and give rise to the long, 14 in. (350 mm), round, slender, tapering leaves. The flowers are inconspicuous and the fruit minute. Manatee grass may form extensive meadows. It was formerly known as *Syringodium filiforme* and *Cymodocea manatorum* Ascherson. It is fully marine.

Shoal grass, Cuban shoal grass *Diplanthera wrightii* (Ascherson)
The rhizomes give rise to short stalks that bear clusters of long, 1 to 16 in. (30-400 mm), narrow 1/16 to ½ in. (1-12 mm) leaves that have several parallel veins. It forms extensive beds in shallow water. It is also known as *Halodule wrightii* Ascherson.

FAMILY HYDROCHARITACEAE

Two-leaf halophila *Halophila baillonis* Ascherson
The rhizomes are slender and sprawling, bearing small, oval or spatula-shaped leaves, usually two in number, with smooth or nearly smooth edges. There are three veins. This small plant grows in quiet, muddy or marly bottoms.

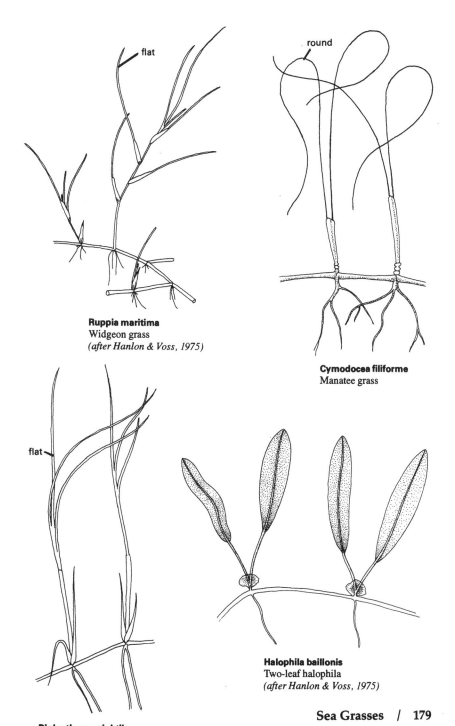

flat

round

Ruppia maritima
Widgeon grass
(after Hanlon & Voss, 1975)

Cymodocea filiforme
Manatee grass

flat

Halophila baillonis
Two-leaf halophila
(after Hanlon & Voss, 1975)

Diplanthera wrightii
Shoal grass
(partly after Correll & Correll, 1972)

Sea Grasses / 179

Six-leaf halophila   *Halophila engelmanni* Ascherson

The sprawling rhizomes give off erect stalks that may be 4 in. (100 mm) high. These bear whorls of usually 6, often 4 to 8, fleshy, elliptical to pointed leaves whose edges are often serrate to scaly. It is not as abundant as *baillonis*.

Turtle grass   *Thalassia testudinum* Koenig & Sims

The rhizomes produce extensive root systems to a depth of over 2 feet (600 mm). The leaves arise in clusters from short stalks. The leaves are flat, ¼ to ¾ in. (4-18 mm) wide and may be 12 in. (300 mm) long. They are finely veined and rounded at the tips. The flowers are large, greenish white to pale pink, and produce prominent seed pods that often wash ashore in considerable numbers along with the ever-present leaves. This grass produces dense meadows of great ecological importance.

Salt Strand Plants

The three species of terrestrial plants described here live at the water's edge and are especially associated with mangrove forests and flood areas.

FAMILY BATACEAE

Saltwort   *Batis maritima* (Linnaeus)

This is a pale green, succulent, spreading shrub. The leaves are thick, usually in pairs, grayish green and pubescent. The flowers are small and borne in the leaf axils. The leaves are 1/5 to 1-1/5 in. (10-30 mm) long and curved upward. The crushed leaves give off a strong scent. It occurs on low shores down to the highwater mark and in mangroves.

FAMILY CHENOPODIACEAE

Glasswort   *Salicornia bigelovii* Linnaeus

The plants are fleshy, shrubby, the branches usually lying prostrate. They form green mats that may turn lead colored or light brown. Bright red spikes are erect and succulent with paired leaves wrapped closely around them. Glasswort grows in the upper intertidal and above on flooded mud or marl flats and are often found in mangroves. They crackle under foot, hence their common name.

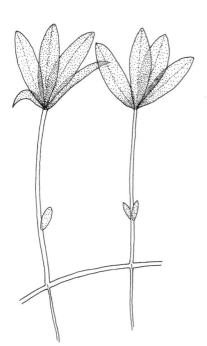

Halophila engelmanni
Six-leaf halophila
(after Hanlon & Voss, 1975)

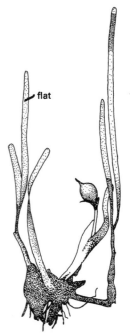

flat

Thalassia testudinum
Turtle grass
(after Hanlon & Voss, 1975)

Batis maritima
Saltwort

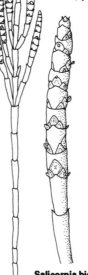

Salicornia bigelovii
Glasswort
(after Correll & Correll, 1972)

Sea Grasses / **181**

FAMILY AIZOACEAE

Sea purslane   *Sesuvium portulacastrum* (Linnaeus)

The plants are sprawling, succulent, with opposite leaves about 1/5 to 2 in. (10-50 mm) long and narrow to slender obovate. They are reddish green or green. The small pink flowers are borne in the leaf axils and have sharp spines or horns on the ends of the petals. *S. maritima* (Walter) is similar but the leaves are shorter, no more than 1 in. (25 mm) long and oblong to spatulate oblong. The flowers are purple. Both species grow at the water's edge.

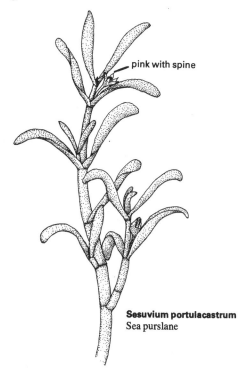

pink with spine

Sesuvium portulacastrum
Sea purslane

The Mangroves

The term mangrove does not apply to a taxonomic division but refers to trees of diverse groups that have adapted to live partially or wholly in saltwater-logged soils in highly saline conditions and that have fruit that germinate or sprout on the tree. They are of great importance to the productivity of tropical waters.

FAMILY COMBRETACEAE

Buttonwood   *Conocarpus erecta* Linnaeus

The buttonwood is a shrub or tree to 60 feet (20 m) tall often with shaggy bark and twisted, gnarled trunks. The leaves are 1 to 4 in. (20-100 mm) long and ovate to elliptical with blunt to sharp tips. The leaves are a pale grayish green. The flowers are greenish. The fruit are conelike and faceted. Buttonwood grows along the beaches near the water's edge. In highly saline conditions they may be stunted to form only low shrubs.

White mangrove   *Laguncularia racemosa* Gaertner

These are shrubs or trees to 60 feet (20 m) tall. The leaves are 2 to 3 in. (40-70 mm) long, oblong to oval with either broadly rounded to indented tips. The leaf stems bear a pair of swollen glands at the base of the leaf. The white mangrove is usually stated to be the inner or shoreward member in the succession from red to black to white mangroves. But whites are often found with buttonwood near the water's edge if the ground is slightly elevated.

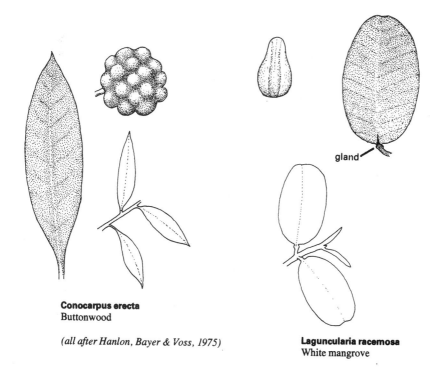

gland

Conocarpus erecta
Buttonwood

(all after Hanlon, Bayer & Voss, 1975)

Laguncularia racemosa
White mangrove

FAMILY RHIZOPHORACEAE

Red mangrove   *Rhizophora mangle* Linnaeus

Trees up to 75 feet (25 m) tall with a gray bark that is red within. The trunks are supported by aerial roots or "prop roots" and long roots descending from the limbs. The leaves are opposite, thick, smooth and leathery, elliptical and bluntly pointed. They are green above and pale below. The yellow flowers give rise to fruit about 1 to 1-1/5 in. (25-35 mm) long that germinate on the tree to form the characteristic long, green, cigar-shaped seedlings. The red mangrove stands in water and flooded flats.

FAMILY AVICENNIACEAE

Black mangrove   *Avicennia germinans* (Linnaeus)

The black mangrove is an erect tree to over 60 feet (20 m) tall with a strong trunk arising directly from the ground. The bark is dark and scaly. The leaves are dark green, oblong to lanceolate elliptical, 1¼ to 5 in. (30-120 mm) long with small, sharp tips often slightly curled. The flowers are white and give rise to elliptical or pointed seeds that sprout on the tree. Characteristic aeration roots or pneumatophores cover the ground under the branches, projecting upward a few inches. These pneumatophores provide an easy and quick method of identification.

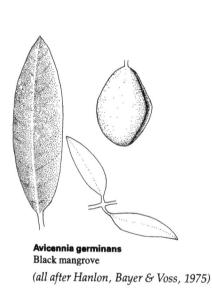

Avicennia germinans
Black mangrove

(all after Hanlon, Bayer & Voss, 1975)

Rhizophora mangle
Red mangrove

Glossary

of less commonly known terms

acute—with narrow sharp tips (spines).

amorphous—without definite or characteristic shape, unorganized.

aperture—any opening, such as the body opening of a snail shell.

articulated—jointed.

axil—angle between a branch or leaf and the axis from which it arises.

bioluminescence—light produced by living organisms, such as that given off by a firefly.

bivalve—member of the molluscan class Pelecypoda; animals having two shells joined by a hinge.

bosses—circular prominences or large round knobs.

Bouin's solution—killing and fixing solution—75 parts of saturated picric acid solution, 25 parts formalin (full strength from the drug store), and 5 parts glacial acetic acid.

branchial—pertaining to the gills.

calcareous—containing calcium carbonate or lime. Usually said of structures that are hardened, such as shells or plates. When the structure is hardened it is said to be calcified.

calcified—stony.

capitulum—rounded head of green alga.

cellulose—polysaccharide constituent of the cell walls of plants and the tests of tunicates.

chitin—tough, flexible, often transparent nitrogenous polysaccharide forming part of the constituents of the exoskeleton of crustaceans and many other invertebrates.

chlorophyll—green photosynthetic pigment of plants.

cilia—(plural of *cilium*) Short, hairlike processes of cells that beat in unison to move the animal about.

circumtropical—found in tropical waters around the world.

commensal—relationship between two animals in which the smaller of the two receives an advantage while the larger one may or may not benefit but is not harmed.

corneous—horny, hornlike.

cosmopolitan—having a nearly worldwide distribution but usually within certain temperature boundaries.

detritus—finely divided debris of organic or inorganic origin.

dichotomous—dividing into two similar parts or branches.

disc — central round plate or cap of brittle stars, basal attachment plate of anemones, barnacles, etc.

drift—line of debris cast onto the beach by waves.

epiphyte—one plant growing on another plant.

filament—delicate threadlike structure.

fucoxanthin—brown carotenoid pigment occurring in brown algae.

gonads—ovaries and testes of animals.

granulose—having granules.

gulf weed—golden brown attached or floating plants of *Sargassum* equipped with berrylike floats.

hermaphrodite—an individual possessing both male and female sexual organs.

holdfast—attachment structure of an alga.

incrusting—growing as a layer on living or nonliving material.

intertidal—region of the shore between the high and low water marks.

invertebrate—animal without a vertebral column.

lappet—a flaplike projection.

larva—stage of an animal when it does not resemble the adult.

lobate, lobal—provided with lobes or arranged in lobes.

maculation—a spotted condition.

mammiform—breast-shaped.

mantle—soft, muscular body wall of brachiopods, mollusks, tunicates, and some other invertebrates.

metamorphosis—abrupt change from the larval stage to juvenile in some animals, such as from the tadpole to the frog.

mucus—slimy, viscous, or lubricating secretion provided by mucous glands.

nodular—covered with little knobs or nodules.

oblique—at an angle from the horizontal or the vertical.

obtuse—with broad or blunt tips (spines).

palp — fleshy tapered or cylindrical projection at the head of polychaete worm. Similar structures are found in other invertebrates.

papilla—(plural, *papillae*) Blunt, rounded or nipple-shaped projections.

peduncle — fleshy stalk by which goose barnacles and brachiopods attach to the substrate.

pelagic—of or pertaining to the open waters of the oceans.

periproct — special plate or membrane on the upper central area of sea urchins bearing the anus.

phycoerythrin—red protein pigment in red algae.

pinnate—featherlike with parts arranged on each side of a main axis.

pinnules—final fine branchlets.

planktonic—pertaining to plankton, the small to minute drifting life in the sea.

plicate—with folds or ridges.

plumose—feathery, with plumes or feathery tips.

polyps—the single attached individuals of colonial or solitary coelenterates.

pore—small to minute round or slitlike opening.

proboscis—cylindrical sensory, offensive, or defensive organ at the anterior end of nemertine worms. Any elongate soft appendage or snout.

pseudopodia — protrusions of protoplasm from the main body of amoeboid protozoans and others used for feeding or locomotion.

pubescent — covered with setae or fine hairs.

pyriform — pear-shaped.

regenerate — to form new body parts when old ones are lost or destroyed.

reproduction — reproduction in invertebrates may be sexual involving males and females, or asexual, by budding, fragmentation of a single individual, transverse fission, or parthenogenesis, the production of young without the union of male and female gametes.

rhizome — horizontal creeping or subsurface stem in seagrasses; similar to stolon in *Caulerpa*.

segmented — divided into various body sections in a linear fashion, as in worms and crustaceans. More advanced animals may also be segmented, though the segments may not be visible in the adult form.

serrate — saw-toothed.

sessile — attached to a substrate either permanently by holdfasts or cement, or by suctorial surfaces. The term is also used for the unstalked barnacles.

seta — (plural, *setae*) Hairlike or needlelike projections of the exoskeleton of crustaceans or in the appendages of polychaete worms.

siliceous — containing silica, a glasslike material.

solitary — an individual organism living separate; distinguished from the more usual organisms of its kind which live in colonies. Solitary coral, solitary tunicate, etc.

spicule — minute calcareous or siliceous bodies forming all or part of the skeleton of many sponges, sea cucumbers, etc.

spinous — bearing spines.

spinules — very small spines.

splash zone — the area just above the high tide mark wetted only by the splashing of waves against the shore.

spray zone — the area just above the splash zone that gets its moisture only from spray. It may extend a considerable distance inland.

stolon — a cylindrical stemlike attachment structure that unites individual animals in some types of colonies. The horizontal stems of plants from which roots and stems arise.

substrate — any solid object, ground, rock, log, etc., to which an animal may attach to or live upon.

succulent — with fleshy tissues (plants) designed to conserve moisture.

suctorial — adapted for sucking or for adhesion.

symbiotic — a close relationship of unicellular plants in the tissues of animals in which both the plants and the animal hosts benefit from the relationship.

thallus — undifferentiated (tissues) plant body as found in algae.

transverse — lying or running across from side to side.

trifurcate — forked into three parts.

tubercle — small, knoblike structure on the skin:

tuberculate — covered with tubercles.

unarmed — a structure which does not bear spines.

vesicles — small, fluid-filled sacs or bladders.

vestige — an organ or part that is small, degenerate, or imperfectly formed and perhaps useless to the organism possessing it.

zooid — a single individual of colonial animals such as hydroids, bryozoa and tunicates.

Selected References

GENERAL

Arnold, Augusta Foote. 1901. The Sea-Beach at Ebb-Tide. The Century Co.
Bayer, Frederick M. and Harding B. Owre. 1968. The Free-living Lower Invertebrates. The Macmillan Company.
Miner, Roy Waldo. 1950. Field Book of Seashore Life. G.P. Putnam's Sons.
Zeiller, Warren. 1974. Tropical Marine Invertebrates of Southern Florida and the Bahama Islands. John Wiley & Sons.

PROTOZOA

Foraminifera

Bock, W.D. 1971. A handbook of the benthonic Foraminifera of Florida Bay and adjacent waters. *In* A Symposium of Recent South Florida Foraminifera. Miami Geological Society Memoir 1.
Cushman, J.A. 1920-1931. The Foraminifera of the Atlantic Ocean. U.S. National Museum, Bull. 104, Parts 1-8.
Hofker, J. 1969. Recent Foraminifera from Barbados. Studies Fauna Curaçao and other Caribbean Islands, Vol. 31.

PORIFERA

de Laubenfels, M.W. 1936. The sponge fauna of the Dry Tortugas. Carnegie Institute of Washington, Publ. No. 30.
_____ 1948. The Order Keratosa of the Phylum Porifera. Occasional Papers of the Allan Hancock Foundation, No. 3.
_____ 1949. Sponges of the western Bahamas. Amer. Museum Novitates No. 1431.
_____ 1953. A guide to the sponges of Eastern North America. Special Publ. Marine Laboratory, University of Miami Press.

COELENTERATA

Hydrozoa

Fraser, C.M. 1944. Hydroids of the Atlantic coast of North America. University Press, Toronto.

van Gemerden-Hoogeveen, G.C. 1965. Hydroids of the Caribbean: Sertulariidae, Plumulariidae and Aglaopheniidae. Studies Fauna Curaçao and other Caribbean Islands. Vol. 22.

Scyphozoa

Hummelinck, P. Wagenaar. 1968. Caribbean Scyphomedusae of the genus *Cassiopea*. Studies Fauna Curaçao and other Caribbean Islands. Vol. 25.

Mayer, A.G. 1910. The Medusae of the World. Vol. 3. Carnegie Institute of Washington Publ. 109.

Anthozoa

Bayer, Frederick M. 1961. The shallow-water Octocorallia of the West Indian region. Studies Fauna Curaçao and other Caribbean Islands. Vol. 12.

Field, L.R. 1949. Sea anemones and corals of Beaufort, North Carolina. Duke University Marine Station. Bull. 5.

Smith, F.G.W. 1948. Atlantic Reef Corals. University of Miami Press. (Second edition 1971).

CTENOPHORA

Mayer, A.G. 1912. Ctenophores of the Atlantic coast of North America. Carnegie Institute of Washington Publ. No. 162.

PLATYHELMINTHES

Hyman, L.H. 1955. Some polyclad flatworms from the West Indies and Florida. Proceedings U.S. National Museum, Vol. 104.

_____ 1955. A further study of the polyclad flatworms of the West Indian region. Bulletin of Marine Science of the Gulf and Caribbean, Vol. 5, No. 4.

NEMERTEA

Coe, W.R. 1900. The Nemerteans of Puerto Rico. Bulletin of the U.S. Fish Commission, Vol. 20, Part 2.

Correa, Diva Diniz. 1961. Nemerteans from Florida and the Virgin Islands. Bulletin of Marine Science of the Gulf and Caribbean, Vol. 11, No. 1.

ANNELIDA

Polychaeta

Ebbs, N. Kenneth, Jr. 1966. The coral-inhabiting polychaetes of the northern Florida reef tract. Part I. Aphroditidae, Polynoidae, Amphinomidae, Eunicidae, and Lysaretidae. Bulletin of Marine Science. Vol. 16, No. 3.

Hartman, Olga. 1951. The littoral marine annelids of the Gulf of Mexico. Publications of the Institute of Marine Science, Texas. Vol. 2, No. 1.

Renaud, J.C. 1956. A report on some polychaetous annelids from the Miami-Bimini area. American Museum Novitates, No. 1812.

Treadwell, A.R. 1921. Leodicidae of the West Indian region. Publications of the Carnegie Institute of Washington. No. 293.

_____ 1939. The polychaetous annelids of Porto Rico and vicinity. Scientific Survey of Puerto Rico and the Virgin Islands. New York Academy of Science, Vol. 16, Part 2.

SIPUNCULIDA

Gerould, J.H. 1913. The sipunculids of the eastern coast of North America. Proceedings of the U.S. National Museum, Vol. 44, No. 1959.

BRYOZOA

Canu, F., and R.S. Bassler. 1928. Fossil and Recent Bryozoa of the Gulf of Mexico. Proceedings of the U.S. National Museum, Vol. 72, Article 14.

Osburn, R.D. 1940. The Bryozoa of Porto Rico, with a résumé of the West Indian Bryozoan fauna. Scientific Survey of Porto Rico and the Virgin Islands. New York Academy of Science, Vol. 16, Part 3.

MOLLUSCA

Abbott, R.T. 1974. American Seashells. Van Nostrand Reinhold. Second edition.

Marcus, E. and E. Marcus. 1967. American opisthobranch mollusks. Studies in Tropical Oceanography, University of Miami Press. Vol. 6.

Voss, Gilbert L. 1956. Review of Cephalopods of the Gulf of Mexico. Bulletin of Marine Science of the Gulf and Caribbean. Vol. 6, No. 2.

Warmke, Germaine L., and R. Tucker Abbott. 1961. Caribbean seashells. Livingston Publishing Co.

ARTHROPODA

Cirripedia

Pilsbry, H.A. 1907. The barnacles contained in the collection of the U.S. National Museum. U.S. National Museum Bulletin 60.

_____ 1916. The sessile barnacles contained in the collections of the U.S. National Museum, including a monograph of the American species. U.S. National Museum Bulletin 93.

Isopoda

Richardson, Harriet. 1905. A monograph of the isopods of North America. U.S. National Museum Bulletin 54.

Decapoda

Chace, Fenner A., Jr. 1972. The shrimps of the Smithsonian-Bredin Caribbean Expeditions, with a summary of the West Indian shallow-water species (Crustacea; Decapoda; Natantia). Smithsonian Contributions to Zoology No. 98.

Holthuis, L.B. 1951. A general revision of the Palaemonidae (Crustacea Decapoda Natantia) of the Americas. I. The subfamilies Euryrhynchinae and Pontoniinae. Occasional Papers of the Allan Hancock Foundation No. 11.

_____ 1952. A general revision of the Palaemonidae (Crustacea Decapoda Natantia) of the Americas. II. The Subfamily Palaemoninae. Occasional Papers of the Allan Hancock Foundation No. 12.

Provenzano, A.J., Jr. 1959. The shallow-water hermit crabs of Florida. Bulletin of Marine Science of the Gulf and Caribbean. Vol. 9, No. 4.

Rathbun, Mary Jane. 1918. The grapsoid crabs of America. U.S. National Museum Bulletin 97.

_____ 1925. The spider crabs of America. U.S. National Museum Bulletin 129.

_____ 1930. The cancroid crabs of America. U.S. National Museum Bulletin 152.

_____ 1937. The oxystomatous and allied crabs of America. U.S. National Museum Bulletin 166.

Schmitt, W.L. 1935. Anomura and Macrura of Porto Rico. Scientific Survey of Porto Rico and the Virgin Islands. New York Academy of Science. Vol. 15, No. 2.

Stomatopoda

Manning, R.B. 1969. Stomatopod Crustacea of the Western Atlantic. Studies in Tropical Oceanography, University of Miami Press. Vol. 8.

ECHINODERMATA

Clark, H.L. 1933. A handbook of the littoral echinoderms of Porto Rico and the other West Indian islands. Scientific survey of Porto Rico and the Virgin Islands. New York Academy of Science. Vol. 16, No. 1.

Downey, Maureen E. 1973. Starfishes from the Caribbean and the Gulf of Mexico. Smithsonian Contributions to Zoology No. 126.

TUNICATA

Van Name, W.G. 1921. Ascidians of the West Indian region and southwestern United States. Bulletin of the American Museum of Natural History. Vol. 45, No. 16.

_____ 1936. The ascidians of Porto Rico. Scientific Survey of Porto Rico and the Virgin Islands. New York Academy of Science, Vol. 10, Part 4.

_____ 1945. The North and South American Ascidians. Bulletin of the American Museum of Natural History No. 84.

ALGAE

Edwards, Peter. 1976. Illustrated guide to the seaweeds and sea grasses in the vicinity of Port Aransas, Texas. University of Texas Press.

Dawes, Clinton J. 1974. Marine algae of the west coast of Florida. University of Miami Press.

Taylor, William Randolph. 1972. Marine algae of the eastern tropical and subtropical coasts of the Americas. University of Michigan Press.

Woelkerling, William J. 1976. South Florida benthic marine algae: keys and comments. University of Miami.

SEA GRASSES, BEACH PLANTS, AND MANGROVES

Hanlon, Roger, Frederick Bayer, and Gilbert Voss. 1975. Guide to the mangroves, buttonwood, and poisonous shoreline trees of Florida, the Gulf of Mexico, and the Caribbean region. Sea Grant Field Guide Series No. 3.

_____ and Gilbert Voss. 1975. A guide to the sea grasses of Florida, the Gulf of Mexico and the Caribbean region. Sea Grant Field Guide Series No. 4.

Index

Index / 193

A CATALOG OF SELECTED

DOVER BOOKS

IN ALL FIELDS OF INTEREST

A CATALOG OF SELECTED DOVER
BOOKS IN ALL FIELDS OF INTEREST

CONCERNING THE SPIRITUAL IN ART, Wassily Kandinsky. Pioneering work by father of abstract art. Thoughts on color theory, nature of art. Analysis of earlier masters. 12 illustrations. 80pp. of text. 5⅜ x 8½.   23411-8

ANIMALS: 1,419 Copyright-Free Illustrations of Mammals, Birds, Fish, Insects, etc., Jim Harter (ed.). Clear wood engravings present, in extremely lifelike poses, over 1,000 species of animals. One of the most extensive pictorial sourcebooks of its kind. Captions. Index. 284pp. 9 x 12.   23766-4

CELTIC ART: The Methods of Construction, George Bain. Simple geometric techniques for making Celtic interlacements, spirals, Kells-type initials, animals, humans, etc. Over 500 illustrations. 160pp. 9 x 12. (Available in U.S. only.)   22923-8

AN ATLAS OF ANATOMY FOR ARTISTS, Fritz Schider. Most thorough reference work on art anatomy in the world. Hundreds of illustrations, including selections from works by Vesalius, Leonardo, Goya, Ingres, Michelangelo, others. 593 illustrations. 192pp. 7⅛ x 10¼.   20241-0

CELTIC HAND STROKE-BY-STROKE (Irish Half-Uncial from "The Book of Kells"): An Arthur Baker Calligraphy Manual, Arthur Baker. Complete guide to creating each letter of the alphabet in distinctive Celtic manner. Covers hand position, strokes, pens, inks, paper, more. Illustrated. 48pp. 8¼ x 11.   24336-2

EASY ORIGAMI, John Montroll. Charming collection of 32 projects (hat, cup, pelican, piano, swan, many more) specially designed for the novice origami hobbyist. Clearly illustrated easy-to-follow instructions insure that even beginning papercrafters will achieve successful results. 48pp. 8¼ x 11.   27298-2

THE COMPLETE BOOK OF BIRDHOUSE CONSTRUCTION FOR WOODWORKERS, Scott D. Campbell. Detailed instructions, illustrations, tables. Also data on bird habitat and instinct patterns. Bibliography. 3 tables. 63 illustrations in 15 figures. 48pp. 5¼ x 8½.   24407-5

BLOOMINGDALE'S ILLUSTRATED 1886 CATALOG: Fashions, Dry Goods and Housewares, Bloomingdale Brothers. Famed merchants' extremely rare catalog depicting about 1,700 products: clothing, housewares, firearms, dry goods, jewelry, more. Invaluable for dating, identifying vintage items. Also, copyright-free graphics for artists, designers. Co-published with Henry Ford Museum & Greenfield Village. 160pp. 8¼ x 11.   25780-0

HISTORIC COSTUME IN PICTURES, Braun & Schneider. Over 1,450 costumed figures in clearly detailed engravings–from dawn of civilization to end of 19th century. Captions. Many folk costumes. 256pp. 8⅜ x 11¾.   23150-X

FRANK LLOYD WRIGHT'S DANA HOUSE, Donald Hoffmann. Pictorial essay of residential masterpiece with over 160 interior and exterior photos, plans, elevations, sketches and studies. 128pp. 9¼ x 10¾. 29120-0

THE MALE AND FEMALE FIGURE IN MOTION: 60 Classic Photographic Sequences, Eadweard Muybridge. 60 true-action photographs of men and women walking, running, climbing, bending, turning, etc., reproduced from rare 19th-century masterpiece. vi + 121pp. 9 x 12. 24745-7

1001 QUESTIONS ANSWERED ABOUT THE SEASHORE, N. J. Berrill and Jacquelyn Berrill. Queries answered about dolphins, sea snails, sponges, starfish, fishes, shore birds, many others. Covers appearance, breeding, growth, feeding, much more. 305pp. 5¼ x 8¼. 23366-9

ATTRACTING BIRDS TO YOUR YARD, William J. Weber. Easy-to-follow guide offers advice on how to attract the greatest diversity of birds: birdhouses, feeders, water and waterers, much more. 96pp. 5³⁄₁₆ x 8¼. 28927-3

MEDICINAL AND OTHER USES OF NORTH AMERICAN PLANTS: A Historical Survey with Special Reference to the Eastern Indian Tribes, Charlotte Erichsen-Brown. Chronological historical citations document 500 years of usage of plants, trees, shrubs native to eastern Canada, northeastern U.S. Also complete identifying information. 343 illustrations. 544pp. 6½ x 9¼. 25951-X

STORYBOOK MAZES, Dave Phillips. 23 stories and mazes on two-page spreads: Wizard of Oz, Treasure Island, Robin Hood, etc. Solutions. 64pp. 8¼ x 11. 23628-5

AMERICAN NEGRO SONGS: 230 Folk Songs and Spirituals, Religious and Secular, John W. Work. This authoritative study traces the African influences of songs sung and played by black Americans at work, in church, and as entertainment. The author discusses the lyric significance of such songs as "Swing Low, Sweet Chariot," "John Henry," and others and offers the words and music for 230 songs. Bibliography. Index of Song Titles. 272pp. 6½ x 9¼. 40271-1

MOVIE-STAR PORTRAITS OF THE FORTIES, John Kobal (ed.). 163 glamor, studio photos of 106 stars of the 1940s: Rita Hayworth, Ava Gardner, Marlon Brando, Clark Gable, many more. 176pp. 8⅜ x 11¼. 23546-7

BENCHLEY LOST AND FOUND, Robert Benchley. Finest humor from early 30s, about pet peeves, child psychologists, post office and others. Mostly unavailable elsewhere. 73 illustrations by Peter Arno and others. 183pp. 5⅜ x 8½. 22410-4

YEKL and THE IMPORTED BRIDEGROOM AND OTHER STORIES OF YIDDISH NEW YORK, Abraham Cahan. Film Hester Street based on *Yekl* (1896). Novel, other stories among first about Jewish immigrants on N.Y.'s East Side. 240pp. 5⅜ x 8½. 22427-9

SELECTED POEMS, Walt Whitman. Generous sampling from *Leaves of Grass*. Twenty-four poems include "I Hear America Singing," "Song of the Open Road," "I Sing the Body Electric," "When Lilacs Last in the Dooryard Bloom'd," "O Captain! My Captain!"—all reprinted from an authoritative edition. Lists of titles and first lines. 128pp. 5³⁄₁₆ x 8¼. 26878-0

PIANO TUNING, J. Cree Fischer. Clearest, best book for beginner, amateur. Simple repairs, raising dropped notes, tuning by easy method of flattened fifths. No previous skills needed. 4 illustrations. 201pp. 5⅜ x 8½. 23267-0

HINTS TO SINGERS, Lillian Nordica. Selecting the right teacher, developing confidence, overcoming stage fright, and many other important skills receive thoughtful discussion in this indispensible guide, written by a world-famous diva of four decades' experience. 96pp. 5⅜ x 8½. 40094-8

THE COMPLETE NONSENSE OF EDWARD LEAR, Edward Lear. All nonsense limericks, zany alphabets, Owl and Pussycat, songs, nonsense botany, etc., illustrated by Lear. Total of 320pp. 5⅜ x 8½. (Available in U.S. only.) 20167-8

VICTORIAN PARLOUR POETRY: An Annotated Anthology, Michael R. Turner. 117 gems by Longfellow, Tennyson, Browning, many lesser-known poets. "The Village Blacksmith," "Curfew Must Not Ring Tonight," "Only a Baby Small," dozens more, often difficult to find elsewhere. Index of poets, titles, first lines. xxiii + 325pp. 5⅝ x 8¼. 27044-0

DUBLINERS, James Joyce. Fifteen stories offer vivid, tightly focused observations of the lives of Dublin's poorer classes. At least one, "The Dead," is considered a masterpiece. Reprinted complete and unabridged from standard edition. 160pp. 5$\frac{3}{16}$ x 8¼. 26870-5

GREAT WEIRD TALES: 14 Stories by Lovecraft, Blackwood, Machen and Others, S. T. Joshi (ed.). 14 spellbinding tales, including "The Sin Eater," by Fiona McLeod, "The Eye Above the Mantel," by Frank Belknap Long, as well as renowned works by R. H. Barlow, Lord Dunsany, Arthur Machen, W. C. Morrow and eight other masters of the genre. 256pp. 5⅜ x 8½. (Available in U.S. only.) 40436-6

THE BOOK OF THE SACRED MAGIC OF ABRAMELIN THE MAGE, translated by S. MacGregor Mathers. Medieval manuscript of ceremonial magic. Basic document in Aleister Crowley, Golden Dawn groups. 268pp. 5⅜ x 8½. 23211-5

NEW RUSSIAN-ENGLISH AND ENGLISH-RUSSIAN DICTIONARY, M. A. O'Brien. This is a remarkably handy Russian dictionary, containing a surprising amount of information, including over 70,000 entries. 366pp. 4½ x 6⅛. 20208-9

HISTORIC HOMES OF THE AMERICAN PRESIDENTS, Second, Revised Edition, Irvin Haas. A traveler's guide to American Presidential homes, most open to the public, depicting and describing homes occupied by every American President from George Washington to George Bush. With visiting hours, admission charges, travel routes. 175 photographs. Index. 160pp. 8¼ x 11. 26751-2

NEW YORK IN THE FORTIES, Andreas Feininger. 162 brilliant photographs by the well-known photographer, formerly with *Life* magazine. Commuters, shoppers, Times Square at night, much else from city at its peak. Captions by John von Hartz. 181pp. 9¼ x 10¾. 23585-8

INDIAN SIGN LANGUAGE, William Tomkins. Over 525 signs developed by Sioux and other tribes. Written instructions and diagrams. Also 290 pictographs. 111pp. 6⅛ x 9¼. 22029-X

CATALOG OF DOVER BOOKS

THE STORY OF THE TITANIC AS TOLD BY ITS SURVIVORS, Jack Winocour (ed.). What it was really like. Panic, despair, shocking inefficiency, and a little heroism. More thrilling than any fictional account. 26 illustrations. 320pp. 5⅜ x 8½. 20610-6

FAIRY AND FOLK TALES OF THE IRISH PEASANTRY, William Butler Yeats (ed.). Treasury of 64 tales from the twilight world of Celtic myth and legend: "The Soul Cages," "The Kildare Pooka," "King O'Toole and his Goose," many more. Introduction and Notes by W. B. Yeats. 352pp. 5⅜ x 8½. 26941-8

BUDDHIST MAHAYANA TEXTS, E. B. Cowell and others (eds.). Superb, accurate translations of basic documents in Mahayana Buddhism, highly important in history of religions. The Buddha-karita of Asvaghosha, Larger Sukhavativyuha, more. 448pp. 5⅜ x 8½. 25552-2

ONE TWO THREE . . . INFINITY: Facts and Speculations of Science, George Gamow. Great physicist's fascinating, readable overview of contemporary science: number theory, relativity, fourth dimension, entropy, genes, atomic structure, much more. 128 illustrations. Index. 352pp. 5⅜ x 8½. 25664-2

EXPERIMENTATION AND MEASUREMENT, W. J. Youden. Introductory manual explains laws of measurement in simple terms and offers tips for achieving accuracy and minimizing errors. Mathematics of measurement, use of instruments, experimenting with machines. 1994 edition. Foreword. Preface. Introduction. Epilogue. Selected Readings. Glossary. Index. Tables and figures. 128pp. 5⅜ x 8½. 40451-X

DALÍ ON MODERN ART: The Cuckolds of Antiquated Modern Art, Salvador Dalí. Influential painter skewers modern art and its practitioners. Outrageous evaluations of Picasso, Cézanne, Turner, more. 15 renderings of paintings discussed. 44 calligraphic decorations by Dalí. 96pp. 5⅜ x 8½. (Available in U.S. only.) 29220-7

ANTIQUE PLAYING CARDS: A Pictorial History, Henry René D'Allemagne. Over 900 elaborate, decorative images from rare playing cards (14th–20th centuries): Bacchus, death, dancing dogs, hunting scenes, royal coats of arms, players cheating, much more. 96pp. 9¼ x 12¼. 29265-7

MAKING FURNITURE MASTERPIECES: 30 Projects with Measured Drawings, Franklin H. Gottshall. Step-by-step instructions, illustrations for constructing handsome, useful pieces, among them a Sheraton desk, Chippendale chair, Spanish desk, Queen Anne table and a William and Mary dressing mirror. 224pp. 8⅛ x 11¼. 29338-6

THE FOSSIL BOOK: A Record of Prehistoric Life, Patricia V. Rich et al. Profusely illustrated definitive guide covers everything from single-celled organisms and dinosaurs to birds and mammals and the interplay between climate and man. Over 1,500 illustrations. 760pp. 7½ x 10⅛. 29371-8

Paperbound unless otherwise indicated. Available at your book dealer, online at **www.doverpublications.com**, or by writing to Dept. GI, Dover Publications, Inc., 31 East 2nd Street, Mineola, NY 11501. For current price information or for free catalogues (please indicate field of interest), write to Dover Publications or log on to **www.doverpublications.com** and see every Dover book in print. Dover publishes more than 500 books each year on science, elementary and advanced mathematics, biology, music, art, literary history, social sciences, and other areas.